THE BRONTËS
Branwell, Anne, Emily, Charlotte

THE BRONTËS

Branwell, Anne, Emily, Charlotte

Bettina L. Knapp

A Frederick Ungar Book

CONTINUUM • NEW YORK

1992

The Continuum Publishing Company
370 Lexington Avenue
New York, NY 10017

Printed in the United States of America

Library of Congress Cataloging-in-Publication Data

Knapp, Bettina Liebowitz, 1926–
    The Brontës : Branwell, Anne, Emily, Charlotte /
    Bettina L. Knapp.
        p.   cm.   — (Literature and life. British writers)
    "A Frederick Ungar Book."
    Includes bibliographical references (p.   ) and index.
    ISBN 0–8264–0514–2 (Cloth)
    1. Brontë family.   2. Brontë, Patrick Branwell, 1817–1848.
3. Brontë, Anne, 1820–1849.   4. Brontë, Emily, 1818–1848.
5. Brontë, Charlotte, 1816–1855.   6. Authors, English—19th
century—Biography.   7. English literature—19th century—
History and criticism.   I. Title.   II. Series.
    PR4168.K6   1991
    823'.809—dc20   90–2554
                                                                  CIP

Contents

Introduction

Why do *Wuthering Heights* and *Jane Eyre* still fascinate and haunt contemporary readers and filmgoers? How is it that Emily and Charlotte Brontë, living in the small and isolated village of Haworth in Yorkshire, in nineteenth-century England surrounded by miles of lonely and wild moors, wrote works whose appeal triggers such eternal and universal responses? Nor should the writings of Anne, the youngest and most neglected of the Brontë sisters, be denied praise. Although not in the same category as *Wuthering Heights* or *Jane Eyre*, Anne's feminist novel, *Agnes Grey*, reflecting the vagaries of difficult personality types, stands on its own. Patrick Branwell, the only boy in the family, although superbly intelligent and well-read in Greek, Latin, history, literature, and other disciplines was not like his sisters. He had neither the stamina nor the self-discipline to think out his writings, preferring to commit onto paper what came easily to him. Emotionally locked in his adolescent narcissistic world, he never succeeded in taking that leap from his juvenilia writings to those of the mature, objective, and thoughtful artist. Weak and self-indulgent, he yielded to alcohol and drugs to assuage his turbulent sense of failure—and died at thirty-one as a result.

What are the elements implicit in the novels of Emily, Charlotte, and Anne that struck deeply into the hearts and minds of both Victorian society and into the modern highly industrialized contemporary world as well? The characters portrayed, the themes probed, the feelings drawn from nature, even the Gothicism of the plots and the architectural constructs in which the action occurs are so authentically portrayed as to draw one inextricably into the folds of the happenings.

Emily, withdrawn and shy, was never able to live away from home for any length of time. If shorn from her nurturing and life-sustaining moors, those savage boggy sedges, that wasteland that was her life, she languished and withered. *Wuthering Heights* fed directly, powerfully, and with urgency from her own viscerality, narrates a primordial experience, a myth—Emily's myth. Like *Tristan and Isolde,* it recounts a timeless story, the birth and burgeoning of a searing love that can lead to union only after death. Emily's archetypal creatures, Catherine and Heathcliff, are living mysteries, enigmatic beings emerging into life as if fated to fulfill some higher purpose. Their lives, revealed in symbols, images, dreams, and preternatural events, rose full-blown from her collective unconscious enticing readers to share in their rich and effulgent fantasy life. *Wuthering Heights* recounts a great love, but also a great cruelty that reveals the dark and savage side of personalities. Emily's contemporaries, longing to be spoon-fed heroes and heroines in all of their pristine purity, could not abide the Evil she served them. The presence of the Anti-Christ in *Wuthering Heights,* they cried out, was anathema. Emily disagreed. Her creatures were presented *whole:* not Light without Darkness; not Good without Evil.

More realistic than *Wuthering Heights, Jane Eyre,* narrates the plight of an orphan girl who, by dint of fortitude, moral rectitude, and a will to succeed, earns happiness. What makes Charlotte's novel utterly contemporary—outside of the portents, dreams, signs, and hallucinatory images throughout—is the role accorded painting. As described in *Jane Eyre* via the medium of art, canvases are seen as the connection between inner and outer worlds; as nonverbal means of expressing a whole subliminal dimension. For psychotherapists, a study of the forms, signs, colors, and the actions delineated in the paintings enable them to fathom what fears and anxieties of the artist have vanished beneath, or have always remained buried beyond the horizon of the rational world. *Jane Eyre* received rave criticisms; it had everything to please—then, as it does now: style, content, and hope in a better future. William Makepeace Thackeray, to whom the novel was dedicated, wrote that he had "lost (or won) a whole day in reading it at the busiest period with the printers ... [It] is the first English [novel] I've been able to read for many a day."[1] Few believed that such a work could have been written by a woman.

Charlotte wrote other novels—*The Professor* and *Shirley*—intriguing, but not of the caliber of *Jane Eyre.* Her last, and perhaps most significant novel, *Villette,* deals with an orphan who struggles to earn economic security and intellectual independence as a teacher in a girls' school in Belgium. While probing the social and class inequities in the novel and the feelings of alienation and depression of the protagonist, there are moments of extraordinary tenderness that are nonexistent in Charlotte's other works. Unforgettable as well are the silhouettes and characterizations of teachers and students living in their closed-circuit school environment. Most importantly, *Villette* fleshes out with utmost candor the fundamental antagonisms existing between Protestantism and Catholicism. Critics of the novel took opposite stances. Matthew Arnold labeled *Villette* "hideous, undelightful, convulsed, constricted . . . one of the most utterly disagreeable books I have ever read." G. H. Lewes, on the other hand, considered it "a work of astonishing power and passion."[2]

The words of Anne Brontë's protagonist in *Agnes Grey,* "I must stand alone," reflect the opinions and feelings of the working women of her day and of today's as well. With "smouldering fire" the author examines the manner in which a governess attempts to deal with willful children whose values are based on money and status and whose parents, misinterpreting what was then the new permissive educational methods, spoil them to a fault. George Moore was unequivocal in his response to *Agnes Grey:* "It was the most perfect prose narrative in English literature."[3]

Anne's second novel, *The Tenant of Wildfell Hall,* is even more daring than *Agnes Grey.* When her protagonist learns of her husband's infidelities, she not only denies him all conjugal rights, but leaves him, taking her son with her. Such acts were unheard of in mid-Victorian times. Even Thackeray would have shunned the inclusion of such ultimatums in his works. "If Anne Brontë, had lived ten years longer," George Moore wrote, "she would have taken a place beside Jane Austen, perhaps even a higher place."[4]

To read and hear the English language as used by the Brontë sisters—with its richness and beauty, its measured classical beats and images, its refreshing simplicity and insights into a world of passion, its depictions of nature in all of its moods—is a feast for the senses and the mind. It allows the reader to slip back in time, to inhabit the world of the landscape painter John Constable, to participate in his cool and scented rural scenes in all of their minute and grandiose manifestations, their sharp scientific observations, and their gentle pathos.

Stalking the pages of the Brontës' writings is that other terrifying, eerie, cruel aspect evoked by phantoms reminiscent of Henry Fuseli's "Nightmare" and those fragmented and alienated beings depicted by twentieth-century artists—Giorgio de Chirico, René Magritte, Marcel Duchamp, Max Ernst, and many more—strangers to their world and ours. When referring to the work of art, Picasso stated: "I do not search, I find."[5]

Chronology

1816 Charlotte Brontë was born on April 21, at Thornton (Yorkshire).

1817 Patrick Branwell Brontë born on June 26, at Thornton (Yorkshore).

1818 Emily Jane Brontë was born on July 30, at Thornton (Yorkshire).

1820 Anne Brontë born at Thornton (Yorkshire). The Brontë family moves to Haworth (Yorkshire) in April, where Reverend Patrick Brontë (1777–1861) is appointed perpetual curate.

1821 Their mother, Mrs. Maria Brontë, dies on September 15.

1824 Brontë children Maria, Elizabeth, Charlotte, and Emily enroll at the Clergy Daughter's School, Cowan Bridge (Lancashire).

1825 Maria dies on May 6, Elizabeth on June 15. Charlotte and Emily return home.

1826 Reverend Brontë brings home twelve wooden soldiers for (Patrick) Branwell. The children begin their imaginative games.

1829 Charlotte and Branwell begin writing the Glass Town and Angria sagas together.

1831 Charlotte enrolls at Miss Wooler's School at Roe Head (Yorkshire) in January. Emily and Anne at home, start writing their Gondal saga together.

1832 Charlotte completes her course of study; returns home in May to tutor her sisters.

1835 Charlotte returns to Roe Head as a teacher. Emily enrolls in Miss Wooler's school at Roe Head (July–October). Her physical decline warrants her return home. Branwell's embarrassment after failing to apply to the Royal Academy of Arts in London. He becomes increasingly dependent on alcohol to assuage his moods of depression.

1836 Anne enrolls at Roe Head where she remains until 1837. Emily's earliest dated poem, July 12.

1837 Emily teaches at Law Hill School, near Halifax, where she remains for about six months.

1838 Charlotte resigns position at Roe Head and returns home. More than half of Emily's surviving poems written between 1838–42.

1839 Anne becomes governess to the Ingham family at Blake Hall in 1839.

1841–45 Anne is governess to the Robinson family at Thorp Green Hall, near York.

1842 In February, Charlotte and Emily enroll at the Pensionnat Héger (Brussels). They return home after the death of Aunt Elizabeth Branwell. Branwell dismissed as assistant clerk in a railway company. He overindulges in alcohol and drugs.

1843 Charlotte returns to Brussels in January to teach English and to study. She falls deeply in love with her teacher, Constantine Héger, director of the Pensionnat. Branwell joins Anne as tutor to the Robinson children.

1844 Charlotte returns home in January. Brontë sisters fail in attempt to start a school in Haworth.

1845 Branwell becomes emotionally involved with Mrs. Robinson and is dismissed.

1846 Publication of *Poems by Currer, Ellis, and Acton Bell*, pseudonyms for Charlotte, Emily, and Anne.

1847 Publication of *Jane Eyre* by Charlotte (Currer Bell); *Wuthering Heights* by Emily (Ellis Bell); and *Agnes Grey* by Anne (Acton Bell).

1848 Publication of *The Tenant of Wildfell Hall,* by Anne Brontë. Death of Branwell on September 24. Death of Emily on December 19.

1849 Death of Anne on May 28. Publication of *Shirley,* by Charlotte.

1853 Publication of *Villette,* by Charlotte.

1854 Charlotte marries Reverend A. B. Nicholls on June 29.

1855 Charlotte dies on March 31.

1857 *The Professor* by Charlotte is published posthumously.

Part I

The Life

1

The Worlds of Branwell, Anne, Emily, and Charlotte Brontë

The home of the Brontës at Haworth Parsonage in Yorkshire was a two-story gray millstone grit house with four rooms on each floor, standing at the top of a steep hill behind the town. Built in 1799, along the simple and stately lines dictated by Georgian architecture, its sturdy foundations and heavily flagged roof resisted the harsh winter winds and snows, and the mists and rains of other seasons. Together with the church and the schoolhouse, the Brontë home formed a triangle, a fourth side opening onto sweeping wild moors. These wastelands of black rock, grasses, and heather altered seasonally in color from a tantalizing purple in August and September to dark brown at other periods. The moors represented joy and liberation for the Brontë children and particularly for Emily, who withered physically and emotionally when away from them.

Not without significance for the Brontës, and perhaps an omen, was the graveyard that surrounded the house and garden. Since sanitary conditions were primitive in the early 1900s and the mortality rate high, one wonders whether, as has been suggested, the decaying bodies buried in the earth polluted the Brontë's water supply, thus paving the way for disease. The graveyard may also be viewed as both a real and symbolic reminder of the virtually continuous presence of Death in their lives.[1]

The strong-willed and optimistic Reverend Patrick Brontë, appointed perpetual curate of Haworth, moved with his wife and six children into the parsonage in 1820. He was certain from the beginning that he would get on with the farmers, workers, and worsted mill owners of the region, even during moments of political and economic unrest. He had heard that the area's rough and blunt population made life difficult for previous curates, but Reverend Brontë, having grown up in hardship, was inured to conflict, isolation, and solitude. Perhaps he even had something in common with the inhabitants of Haworth: a spirit of fierce independence and resistance to authority. He did not, therefore, regard negatively the poor roads preventing communication between one town and the next, particularly during the seemingly endless snow-covered winter months. Such insularity had its positive side: it forced the family—and particularly the children—to rely upon themselves for entertainment.

A native of County Down in Northern Ireland, and one of ten children of a farming couple, Reverend Brontë was brought up on hard work and poverty. After a short period of schooling, he became a weaver. Handsome, diligent, intelligent, and ambitious, he early understood that if he were to progress in life he would have to leave his virtually illiterate family. Before doing so, he began teaching at the Glascar Hill Presbyterian School, after which he most probably studied with Reverend Tighe, while also tutoring the reverend's son. It was Tighe, it is thought, who introduced Patrick Brontë to the itinerant Pietist, John Wesley, whose doctrine stressed humankind's sinfulness as well as the notions of personal purity and salvation through Christ. Studying hard and well, Brontë, with the backing of his patron, surmounted the usual social and economic hurdles and enrolled at St. John's College at Cambridge. After earning a BA, he took holy orders in 1806, was ordained to the Methodist-Evangelical group at Wethersfield and Wellington in Shropshire, and then to the manufacturing town of West Riding in Yorkshire (1811–12). Although busy ministering, he still found time to publish the first of his four books of poetry and fiction. The future looked bright for this charismatic Wesleyan-Methodist evangelical minister. He believed in reforming the Church of England from within, in hymn singing, group meetings, and in the "glorious" thought of salvation for all.

Reverend Brontë married the charming and pretty thirty-year-old Maria Branwell from Penzance (Cornwall) in 1812. Penzance's mild climate and palm trees were the antithesis of the grim, austere, cold, bleak winters of Thornton in Yorkshire, where Reverend Brontë was now ministering. Maria was a devout Methodist, as were all the members of her family. She was also well educated and deeply involved with the revival of "serious religion."[2] She saw eye to eye with her husband on political and religious issues such as keeping the Sabbath, family prayer, and the evangelical need to write.

The letters she addressed to her future husband "whom I love beyond all others,"[3] were a blend of Evangelical missionism and passion, in which she confessed her feelings freely. Shortly before their marriage, she writes:

I am certain no one ever loved you with an affection more pure, constant, tender, and ardent than that which I feel. Surely this is not saying too much; it is the truth, and I trust you are worthy to know it. I long to improve in every religious and moral quality, that I may be a help, and if possible an ornament to you. Oh let us pray much for wisdom and grace to fill our appointed stations with propriety, that we may enjoy satisfaction in our own souls, edify others, and bring glory to the name of Him who has so wonderfully preserved, blessed, and brought us together.[4]

Maria Brontë bore six children in seven years: Maria (1813), Elizabeth (1815), Charlotte (1816), Patrick Branwell (1817), Emily (1818), Anne (1820). Still weak from her last and most difficult pregnancy, she made the day-long journey from Thornton to Haworth in a cart, arriving debilitated and in pain from the illness that would lead to her death nine months later. Whether her ailment was cancer or a blood infection resulting from poor postpartum care is not known. Unable to tend to the home or the children, and with no one to nurse his bedridden wife, Reverend Brontë wrote to Maria's elder sister, Elizabeth Branwell. He asked the forty-nine-year-old spinster to come to Haworth. She did so, remaining with the family until her death.

Mrs. Brontë died September 15, 1821 and desolation settled onto the household. The somber atmosphere during Mrs. Brontë's protracted illness increased to despair after her death, particularly for Reverend Brontë. Bereavement seemed to work intensely on the children's spirits as their father became increasingly reclusive, to the extent of dining alone in his study. His continuous activities within the parish—Evangelical and Wesleyan missionary zeal, pastoral care—kept him from being submerged by morbid thoughts. His fervor was such that by 1832 he succeeded in finding funds to build the first Sunday school in Haworth and to buy the first organ and the first bell for the church of St. Michael and All Angels Church. He concerned himself with health problems, seeking to curb disease by requiring the less fortunate inhabitants of Haworth to whitewash their cottages. He attempted to remedy the water supply and drainage systems that had been blamed for the high disease rate in the community. Questions of law and order also came to the reverend's attention.

Because of Reverend Brontë's class consciousness and educational values, he cut his six children off from the companionship of others. The Brontës had little contact with outsiders, except for a few families—namely, those of the church's trustees. Prevented from mingling with the workers or other uneducated folk, the children clung to each other. Constant sounds in their immediate environment, the tolling of funeral bells and the chipping of the gravestone cutter, may have added to their melancholy.

Isolation, howver, served to develop the children's imaginations. They gave rein to fancy, particularly in winter, when daylight hours were short, compelling them to spend much time in the home. They created a separate world of romance, adventure, love, battles, and eerie escapades that they enacted, narrated, or, when older, wrote down.

They discovered early in life that they could not count on their father's company to relieve their loneliness or the monotony of their existence. Aunt Branwell, although righteous, pious, and efficient in household affairs could not assume the role of mother figure in the children's hearts. She was frugal in her habits—a commendable trait for the parson and his family—and was equally abstemious in her emotions. She did not know how to dispense the gentleness and kindness required of a surrogate mother. This role was played by the seven-year-old and deeply religious Maria who appeared to be the perfect incarnation of a nurturing, warm, and thoughtful parent. She was endowed with extraordinary feeling and love for her siblings and brother and was also possessed of a remarkable intelligence. In fact, Reverend Brontë was so impressed with Maria's rare mental gifts that he treated her as though she were an adult. Not only did he trust her with correcting proofs of one of his long poems, but he had her read the parliamentary debates in the papers that he would then discuss with her. Later, Maria would go up to the small second-floor room, where she regaled the younger children with the issues of the day, thus entertaining and educating them as well as keeping them quiet. Thanks to this rare creature, the precocious and self-contained children bestowed their affections and love upon Maria, happily playing together as a harmonious unit.

Reading books, aside from the Bible that was their daily fare, magazines, and newspapers, was one of the children's most precious pastimes. Free access to their father's library, which contained among other works *The Arabian Nights,* John Bunyan's *Pilgrim's Progress, The Methodist Magazine, Blackwood's Magazine, The Times,* the writings of Byron, Wordsworth, Scott, Southey, and Ossian, instilled in the young Brontës an intense desire to learn. The artworks—mostly the apocalyptic engravings of John Martin depicting heavenly realms as real as earthly ones—hung on the walls of the parsonage also served to catalyze their imaginations. Amazingly, when Charlotte was but thirteen, she mentions the names of Guido Reni, Titian, Raphael, Michelangelo, Correggio, Leonardo da Vinci, Rubens, Sir Anthony Vandyke, and many more. Needless to say, the Brontë children's superior knowledge, though not always systematic and methodically acquired, served increasingly to cut them off from the untutored, thus isolating them still further.

After two years of widowhood, Reverend Brontë made some effort to find a suitable wife. Twice rejected, he finally decided to expend his energies by increasing his work load in the parish. He visited the sick even more assiduously than before; he supervised school programs and performed evangelical work.

As his children grew older, he spent long hours tutoring them in history, French, and Latin. Most of his time was given over to the education of Branwell, as he was called, his only son, his pride and joy, most favored by him as well as by his daughters. By the age of ten Branwell had been taught ancient and modern history, Greek and Latin, and had read the works of Homer and Virgil. Reverend Brontë did more than teach his children; he endowed them with a spirit of inquiry and integrity and an enthusiasm for learning. He instilled in them a willingness to die for the spiritual truths in which they believed. He encouraged them to maintain their own ideas even though these might differ from majority opinion. Reverend Brontë was not a Calvinist. He had adopted Wesleyan Methodism with its conviction of personal salvation through Jesus Christ and conversion revolving around the "warming of the heart." Nevertheless he emphasized, both at home and in his Sunday sermons, that hell and damnation awaited sinners. Perhaps the religious crisis undergone by Charlotte, Branwell, and Anne during their teens was caused in part by the terror of fire and brimstone awaiting the sinful and the impure of heart and body.

From their earliest years the reverend's daughters realized that a parson's stipend was low and that money was and always would be scarce in the Brontë household. They would have to rely on themselves for economic support. Education was crucial for a post as governess or teacher, the only two careers open to women who did not want to be housemaids, so they would have to plan a course of study for themselves. Maria and Elizabeth were sent to the Clergy Daughters' School at Cowan Bridge in July 1824; Charlotte followed in August, and Emily in November. Although the two older sisters had just recovered from whooping cough and measles, they were considered strong enough to make the fifty-mile journey and expected to perform well at the charity school. Perhaps Reverend Brontë did not fully realize the extent of the physical privations, the meagerness and poor quality of the food, and the harshness of the discipline at the school, where scrofula was rampant.

Brought up to admire freedom of thought and considering themselves far above average in learning, the Brontë girls were shocked to discover their deficiencies in certain disciplines, and especially in the rules of grammar. Maria and Elizabeth became scapegoats, often accused of daydreaming, and were persecuted for their deficiencies in housewifery. Unsanitary conditions (one stone privy for sixty girls and the staff), overcrowded sleeping quarters, extreme dampness, and cold added dangerously to the unpleasant circumstances with which they had to contend. Even when Maria became seriously ill, she was forced to go about her school activities and obligations as usual. By April, before the outbreak of typhoid and typhus epidemics, Maria was taken home, diagnosed with galloping consumption, a disease that devastated so many nineteenth-century households. Elizabeth was sent back to Haworth Parsonage suffering from the same sickness in May. Maria died on May 6; Elizabeth on June 15. Only then were Charlotte and Emily brought home immediately.

Reverend Brontë wrote that Maria "exhibited during her illness many symptoms of a heart under divine influence."[5] He was devastated. The children, and most particularly Branwell, were overwhelmed with sorrow: they had lost Maria, their precious surrogate mother. This proved to be far more excoriating than the loss of their real mother because her death had occurred when they were too young to understand such dispossession. They now had to learn to face bereavement. Never did they recover from the loss of Maria, a virtually sacred power in their lives. Her presence was imprinted in their poetry, in their juvenilia, as well as in their later works, just as gravity was imprinted henceforth on their features. The tombstones of their mother and sisters were visible from every window of the house, a daily reminder of their losses.

The Brontë children now associated the world beyond Haworth—that of school—with ominous and threatening forces and disruptive energies: the destruction of love and security. Only within the parsonage and the surrounding moors was the world safe, or so it seemed.

Charlotte, as the eldest now, assumed the mothering role, although she was never able to replace the children's adored Maria. She and Miss Branwell shared the responsibilities of the household. Together they taught the girls to clean, cook, sew, and make samplers. A new face now entered the Brontë household: Tabitha Aykroayd (the children called her Tabby). This fifty-six-year-old maid was shrewd, practical, and loving. She was a Methodist who knew how to discipline children but also she understood how to regale them with treats. She delighted in surprising them with special foods from her warm kitchen and in telling them wonderfully exciting stories in her Yorkshire dialect.

A memorable date for the Brontë children was June 1826. Their father returned from a brief visit to Leeds bringing Branwell (Brannii as the family called him) a box of twelve new wooden soldiers to replace the worn-out ones of two years before. Using Branwell's soldiers as props, the children wrote poems, plays, and dramatic stories based on the lives of heroic figures. When he now offered each of his sisters one of the "Young Men," as he called his new soldiers, Charlotte's choice fell on "the Duke of Wellington"; Emily's grave-looking adventurer was to be known as "Gravey"; Anne's, with his peculiar air, was "Waiting-Boy"; while Branwell christened his, "Buonaparte."[6]

Excitement pervaded the atmosphere as the soldiers went on their new and daredevil adventures. Days, weeks, and years were spent creating an incredible collection of juvenilia, including plays that they performed at home, poems that they read aloud, magazine articles that they wrote and illustrated, and sagas of all types, which were committed to paper in tiny letters, not only in an endeavor to replicate printed volumes, but also to maintain great secrecy. They wanted no one in the household to peer into their private world. Indeed, the exploits of the fearless Brontë soldiers took them on dangerous exploratory missions to the mouth of the Niger, on the northwest coast of Africa, where they founded their Glass Town Confederacy.

The creators of these mind-boggling sagas were none other than the Genii inspired by the *Arabian Nights,* namely, Branwell, Chief Genius Brannii; Charlotte, Chief Genius Tallii; and the two younger ones, Emmii and Annii Branwell. Branwell, the poet, was responsible for the maps and the new language spoken by the valiant "Young Men." With the passing of years, the stories took on greater amplitude, becoming more and more complicated, a veritable network of colonizations, romantic interludes, and heroic battles.

Characters, both historical and fictional, were added or deleted; names were changed and what had once been dubbed Glass Town became known as the more elegant Verdopolis, and still later, as Angria. Although the children were inspired by a variety of works they had read, the passionate and heroic rebel, outcast, and fighter for causes, Lord Byron, was their absolute favorite.

Several months after Reverend Brontë had recuperated from a severe inflammation of the lungs, which had left him greatly weakened, the children's creative lives changed in 1831. Their father decided that if his daughters were to earn livelihoods as governesses, they must be further educated and in a traditional school manner. The fifteen-year-old Charlotte was sent to Roe Head School, twenty miles away from Haworth, directed by the Misses Wooler.

Since Charlotte still associated her sisters' deaths with the outside world, to be away from home, even nearby Roe Head was terrifying to her. Her fear of school was compounded by her self-image of plainness: short, fragile, long thick brown hair, almond-shaped eyes, a large nose, and "crooked mouth." Despite her fear and trepidation, and her innate and perhaps pathological shyness, Charlotte was determined to achieve her goal and learn as much as she could. Her "expression was of quiet, listening intelligence; but now and then, on some just occasion for vivid interest or wholesome indignation, a light would shine out, as if some spiritual lamp had been kindled, which glowed behind those expressive orbs."[7] Unlike the harsh headmistress of the first school she had attended, the directors of Roe Head were the kind, motherly Miss Margaret Wooler and her three spinster sisters. They kept the two floors devoted to school affairs and classrooms, for their seven to ten students, pleasant and sunny. The third floor of Roe Head remained unoccupied, "except by the ghostly idea of a lady, whose rustling silk gown was sometimes heard by the listeners at the foot of the second flight of stairs." Perhaps the Gothic atmosphere of Roe Head inspired the haunting and fearful attic sequences in Charlotte's novels, *Jane Eyre* and *Villette*.

Charlotte's adaptation to Roe Head's intellectual standards was difficult and painful. Brought up by her father to believe she was far above average in intelligence and in learning, and to be told by Miss Wooler that she was deficient in grammar and would have to be placed in the less advanced class, was so traumatic that she wept. Sensitive to Charlotte's emotional needs and aware of her ambitious nature Miss Wooler realized that it would be more productive to place her in the first class and permit her to make up her inadequacies by studying longer hours and privately. In some disciplines, however, such as literature, history, and politics, Charlotte confounded her teachers by the breadth and sweep of her knowledge. That her intellectual performance gradually proved exceptional and that she was admired by teachers and peers alike, make it difficult to account for Charlotte's extreme shyness and depression. Was it because her tuition was paid by the Atkinsons, her father's friends, thus categorizing her, as at Cowan Bridge, a charity case? A clear distinction marked Charlotte from other students, who came from relatively affluent homes of manufacturing families. Their ways were as different from hers as were their clothes, and even their accents—Charlotte's being heavily Irish. Other factors may also explain Charlotte's feelings of alienation. Accustomed to relative reclusion, she now found herself in competition with others—socially, economically, and intellectually—which served to accentuate her already pronounced inferiority complex. Although her suffering was intense, Charlotte was of strong mettle: an "indefatigable student," thoughtful and analytical in her approach to learning. Rather than linger in despair, she concentrated her efforts on grammar, geography, literature, drawing, piano, and French.

Still, something was amiss at Roe Head. Despite the warm and congenial atmosphere the Misses Wooler created for her, Charlotte was not only deeply homesick, but dwelled on her two departed sisters, Maria and Elizabeth, talking and dreaming about them obsessively. So disturbing was one of Charlotte's dreams that when Miss Wooler asked her to tell her about it, she at first refused. Only when coaxed did she describe the content: she dreamt she was "told that she was wanted in the drawing-room, and it was Maria and Elizabeth." But "it did not go on nicely . . . they were changed . . . they had forgotten what they used to care for. They were very fashionably dressed, and began criticising the room, etc."[8]

Clearly, the dream reveals a sense of estrangement and of painful and virtually insurmountable feelings of divisiveness within Charlotte's psyche. The moat separating her from the other students was one which she could fill neither outwardly nor inwardly. That Maria and Elizabeth wore fashionable dresses instead of the trim, simple, but old-fashioned garb acceptable at the parsonage indicated a projection on to her sisters of traits she might have wanted to emulate for the sake of conformity in order to make life easier for herself. The very thought of such self-indulgence terrified her. Lax conduct would surely lead to perdition, to a loss of identity and of everything for which she stood and had been taught to admire, to a contamination of integrity, beauty, and light—characteristics of the saintly Maria and Elizabeth. If the values she prized so highly and considered her own were to be displaced for the sake of expediency, merely to please the majority, that would indicate her renunciation of the legacy left her by her sisters and her family. Conformity to a world dominated by wealth and outer trappings was far too excoriating a thought to articulate openly; therefore, it had been relegated in symbol form to the dream. Interestingly, in Charlotte's novels— *Jane Eyre, Shirley,* or *Villette*—she makes a point of having her heroines dress not as others do, but as is suitable to her nature and temperament. Charlotte was always adamant in retaining her own identity, no matter the circumstances.

Upon completion of three terms at Roe Head, Charlotte had not only studied hard and learned a great deal, but had also earned the respect of classmates and teaching staff alike, thus building her self-confidence. For the first time in her life, she had become friendly with two students—outsiders—whose friendship would be maintained for the rest of her days: Mary Taylor, from a radical and nonconformist family, and Ellen Nussey, volatile, argumentative, and deeply interested in politics.

No sooner had she returned home than Charlotte began instructing her sisters with diligence and fervor:

In the morning, from nine o'clock till half-past twelve, I instruct my Sisters and draw; then we walk till dinner, after dinner I sew till tea time, and after tea I either read, write, do a little fancy work or draw, as I please. Thus, in one delightful, though somewhat monotonous course my life is passed.[9]

During Charlotte's absence from the parsonage she had grown more independent and, to a certain extent, more removed from her family. Although she pursued her writing as before and her swashbuckling protagonists remained essentially Byronic, as attested to in "The Foundling," and "Something about Arthur," she seemed to be searching for more than what was contained in her siblings' juvenilia. Did she want to create something of her own, thus cutting off the symbiotic relationship she had always enjoyed with her brother? Clearly, Charlotte was maturing, while Branwell remained the eternal adolescent.

Perhaps more than Emily and Anne, Branwell was to suffer the consequences of Charlotte's absence. Although they wrote each other assiduously, exchanging ideas about the explorations and exploits of their heroes and heroines, the harmonious relationship existing among the four prior to Charlotte's departure soon altered. Emily and Anne had perhaps grown tired of the Glass Town, Verdopolis, and Angrian sagas; or they might have resented being dominated by the elder two. Taking advantage of Charlotte's absence, they decided to leave Branwell to his own devices, joining together to create their own world of fantasy, orally at first, then, after 1835, committing to paper their own complex epics revolving around Gondal, an imaginary island in the north Pacific. Their active, dramatic, and dangerous explorers, setting out for the unknown, also colonized Gaaldine, an island in the south Pacific.

While the imaginery world of the Gondalians fulfilled the needs and desires of the two younger sisters, Branwell's creative life during Charlotte's absence and after her return was experienced so intensely that the empirical world was relegated to second place. By devoting every free moment to sketching, painting, drawing views of the new lands discovered by his heroes, he lived out their blood-and-thunder adventures as outcasts, pirates, soldiers of fortune, idealists, conquerors, or murderers. The vicarious excitement he enjoyed during the illustration and writing process filled him with such incredible energy that, like a drug, it yielded him a false sense of accomplishment. Still, a perusal of the juvenilia of the four Brontës produces marvel at the fertility and resourcefulness of their young minds. Equally astounding were their intellectual attainments and their knowledge of politics, military science, history, geography, poetry, classics, music, and art.

Difficult times were ahead for the Brontës as a family, and for Branwell in particular. Apart from an alleged short period at the Haworth Grammar School, he was the only Brontë offspring not to be educated away from home. Was it because he was a delicate undersized child? Could his father have feared that, despite his son's good looks, his red hair might have caused him to become a butt of ridicule? Was it because of his poor sight? He wore corrective glasses at an early age, but the required reading and the sharing of books might prove to be a strain on his sight. Or was it because he considered his son superior to the other lads attending country schools and believed he might learn better at home? The father's reasons for keeping him at home are still uncertain.

One may wonder today whether studying Greek, Latin, history, and other disciplines with his father on a daily basis was psychologically sound. Were the expectations of the highly disciplined and awesome reverend not too great? Did Branwell fear, unconsciously, that he would never be able to live up to his father's standards? Is it any wonder then, that during the lad's hours of leisure, he should seek solace in his world of fantasies where he was lord and master of his creations? There, he could lead his heroic and bloody conquests, direct the actions of his passionate characters whose visions of the world were often more villainous and ignominious than saintly.

Another problem haunted Branwell. He had always felt Maria's death more heartrendingly than had his sisters. As the one and only *real* mother figure in his life, she had been his mainstay and support, enabling him to counteract what he experienced as increasingly burdensome to him—his father's expectations. Over and over again in his narratives and poems, he reveals his intense need for love and understanding, which seems to grow in proportion to his diminishing self-image.

> I must never look on thee—
> If there's no God, no Heaven, no Hell,
> Thou within thy grave must dwell—
> I, left blackening in the storm—
> Both a banquet for the worm.

Not only did Maria's death leave a void in Branwell's heart, but under his aunt's religious tutelage and her emphasis on sin he developed a sense of intolerable guilt and unworthiness. As he grew older, he began questioning the very existence of love and of compassion in the Godhead itself. If Maria, who was perfection, was killed by God, what would *his* fate be? Because he could in no way measure up to her purity and beauty of soul, he was fated to become a pariah and an outcast. The notion of sin, coupled with his own sense of unworthiness, became instrumental in Branwell's falling away from religion and doubting the very existence of God. In church on Sundays, he would choose a pew near the window where, unobserved, he would read not a Prayer Book, but a volume of his choice. Given his strict upbringing, could Branwell, the nonbeliever, be relieved of guilt? Or was he masking harrowing terror, imprisoned by a fearsome sense of sin that would bring divine retribution? Would his rebellion, centering on his disbelief in God, be aimed in reality against his well-meaning father and the high standards set for him? Would such a stand help him break away from his home and cast his own net in the world? Or would guilt overpower him and paralyze his every effort?

Only when decanting his fantasies in flights of imagination did Branwell's excitable nature find release from the increasing burden of empirical reality. By verbalizing his hallucinatory visions, he allowed his overwrought temperament to find release. Unlike Charlotte's passionately romantic and even voluptuous characters forever in and out of love affairs, who were, in the last analysis, relatively rational in their outlook, the creatures of Branwell's fantasy were never well developed. Nor did he attempt, as had Charlotte, Emily, and Anne in their cycles, to find alternative means for his heroes to reach their goals. Never did they use their willpower, for example, to restrain their actions, or rely on integrity and virtue to be their guides. Brutality dominated. The *easy* way out was the course he chose for his protagonists to gain their ends: killing and violence obliterated whatever was problematic and obstructive. To resort to the intellect in order to find alternative routes would have required greater effort on his part, greater patience and perseverance. Moreover, since writing came so easily to Branwell—words just cascaded forth; he was a "genius" to his family—there was no reason either to polish his writing or find other ways of solving his protagonists' difficulties. The world of expediency was his.

Had Reverend Brontë or had Branwell's sisters been aware of the incipient psychological split within the young man's weakly structured ego, Branwell might have been sent to school if only to learn to deal with the rough-and-tumble of the real world, rather than kept cloistered as the household pet. Branwell's narcissistic and self-indulgent comportment was manifested in his need to dominate at least in his writings. His already highly strung temperament became increasingly overwrought, as his nervousness and temper tantrums increased.

The time was fast approaching for the Brontë children—even Branwell—to have to begin thinking seriously about going out into the world to work. Since Reverend Brontë, now turning sixty and not in the best of health, could not afford to give his daughters a substantial dowery, they would probably remain unmarried, and therefore need jobs. When in 1835 Miss Wooler asked Charlotte to return to Roe Head School as a teacher, she accepted, not only for the modest salary, but even more importantly, for Miss Wooler's offer of free education to one of Charlotte's sisters. Emily, the next in line, would accompany Charlotte.

The most beautiful of the Brontë daughters, Emily was "a tall, long armed girl, more fully grown than her elder sister." Her "kind, kindling, liquid eyes" were arresting; their color ranging from dark gray to dark blue, depending upon her mood, spelled reserve.[10] There was, nevertheless, a mysterious unfathomable, ambiguous, and haunting side to her nature: a whole instinctual earth realm that no one had or ever would succeed in penetrating. Intense joy and abandon were hers when running recklessly or rambling carelessly and freely through the ever exhilarating and intensely satisfying moors. In winter or in summer, with or without her sisters, she spent hours inhaling the clean crisp air tinged with the aroma of heather in summer, or wet with the icy snows of winter. She warmed to the variegated and dramatic colorations cast by the ever mobile sun rays, which set forth the surrounding arched hills or deeply creviced cliffs in sharply delineated configurations on cloudless days. Nature spelled life for her in all of its never-ending dimensions and in each of her personifications of its elements. How would such a free soul as Emily's fare in the restrictive and structured school environment?

Emily's separation or cutting off from deeply nurturing factors brought on feelings of acute homesickness. Moreover, the freedom she had enjoyed in her home despite its restrictive atmosphere of virtual seclusion and hushed silence, was, nevertheless, a source of comfort to her. In addition to her beloved moors, there was Tabby, and her kitchen with its wealth of aromas ranging from those of baking bread and muffins, to the multiple fragrances of her soups. Significant as well were those hours Emily devoted to the writing of her Gondal poems. Charlotte was aware of the fact that when away from home, the lack of security and sense of well-being was detrimental to her sister's body/psyche, and wrote:

My sister Emily loved the moors. Flowers brighter than the rose bloomed in the blackest of the heath for her;—out of a sullen hollow in the bleak solitude many and dear delights; and not the least and best-loved was—liberty. Liberty was the breath of Emily's nostrils; without it she perished.[11]

The structure and discipline, although not rigorous at Roe Head, coupled with the lack of privacy, characteristic of a boarding school, brought on Emily's severe depression. Fearing for her health, Charlotte noted:

Every morning when she woke, the vision of home and the moors rushed on her, and darkened and saddened the day that lay before her. Nobody knew what ailed her but me—I knew only too well. In this struggle her health was quickly broken: her white face, attenuated form, and failing strength threatened rapid decline. I felt in my heart she would die, if she did not go home, and with this conviction obtained her recall.[12]

At the month's end, Emily left the school and Anne took her place. Although the return to Haworth meant additional household chores, these were joyfully met, experienced as a release from imprisonment. "I hear my dungeon bars recoil," she wrote in one of her Gondal poems. Her strength restored, Emily flourished.

Anne, considered the most delicate of the Brontë sisters, lived more strongly in the workaday world than Emily. Intransigent, unwilling to waver from what she considered truth, and intent upon helping others in her kind way, Anne was pleased at the prospect of joining Charlotte at Roe Head. Perhaps her vision of right and wrong helped her face the many disappointments and tragedies of the past and those in store for her and her family. Unlike Emily, who fled companionship or friendship with anyone

but her sisters, Anne dreamt of one day getting married and becoming a mother. She yearned for love and knew how to dispense
it appropriately. In her poem, "Dreams," love is viewed as a kind
of epiphany:

> But then to wake and find it flown,
> The dream of happiness destroyed;
> To find myself unloved, alone,
> What tongue can speak the dreary void!
>
> A heart whence warm affections flow,
> Creator, Thou hast given to me;
> And am I only thus to know
> How sweet the joys of love would be?

In the spring of 1837, Miss Wooler, anxious to be closer to her
parents, moved Roe Head School from its high ground site at
Mirfield Moor to the low-lying and damp Dewsbury Moor. Perhaps the change of climate in addition to an increasing work load
caused Charlotte to become emotionally distraught. A sense of
unworthiness and guilt feelings corroded her psyche.

I *do* wish to be better than I am. I pray fervently sometimes to be made
so. I have stings of conscience—visitings of remorse—glimpses of Holy,
inexpressible things, which formerly I used to be a stranger to. It may all
die away, I may be in utter midnight, but I implore a Merciful Redeemer
that if this be the real dawn of the Gospel, it may still brighten to perfect
day. Do not mistake me, Ellen, do not think I am good, I only wish to be
so, I only hate my former flippancy and forwardness. O! I am no better
than I ever was. I am in that state of horrid, gloomy uncertainty. . . . If I
could only thereby ensure the prospect of reconcilement to God and Redemption through His Son's merits.[13]

Charlotte lived her religious crisis on a more emotional level
than Anne, who was also to sustain hers, but with additional
physical repercussions. Ill with severe gastritis and fearful of
death, Anne asked James de la Trobe, a Moravian minister, to
help her through her anguish. In warm and healing terms, he
spoke of love to her rather than of sin emphasized by Reverend
Brontë, thus healing her, at least for the time being. Charlotte,
however, half-crazed with fear that Anne, as her sisters Maria and
Elizabeth, might be suffering from galloping consumption, "up-

braided" Miss Wooler for her coldness, insensitivity, and indifference to her sister's condition. In her biography of Charlotte, the well-known novelist, Mrs. Elizabeth Gaskell notes:

Charlotte watched over her younger sisters with the jealous vigilance of some wild creature, that changes her very nature if danger threatens her young. Anne had a slight cough, a pain at her side, a difficulty of breathing.[14]

After nearly three years as teacher at Roe Head, Charlotte, perhaps overworked, certainly unsuited to the discipline and restrictions of school and the incredible amount of work heaped upon her, nearly suffered a breakdown. Usually self-controlled, she had become extremely tense, shuddering and trembling at the slightest sudden noise, barely able to repress her screams. "My health and my spirit had utterly failed me, and the medical man whom I consulted enjoined me, as I valued my life, to go home."[15] Charlotte lamented the fact that she not only had virtually no time for writing, but had lost the enthusiasm crucial for creativity. Dismayed by Charlotte's accusations and complaints, Miss Wooler wrote to Reverend Brontë, who sent for his children. Charlotte was determined that neither she nor any of her sisters would ever return to Roe Head.

To Charlotte's guilt at not having succeeded as a teacher and at having lost her minuscule salary, was added a harrowing religious crisis. Her narrative, "Passing Events," begun on her twentieth birthday (April 21, 1836) and completed eight days later, focuses on the Calvinist doctrine of predestination and its tenet of eternal damnation for the condemned outcast. Would she be rejected because she had not fulfilled her mission or because she had been unable to provide her family with the necessary funds to keep the household solvent? Would she be fated to Hell?[16] Charlotte's poignant concern over Anne's delicate state of health was compounded by the change in Branwell's behavioral patterns. His conduct with the town boys—now that his father had given him permission to spend time with them—and the evenings spent at the bar of the Black Bull Hotel were sources of concern. So, too, were his membership in the boxing club and his jaunts to neighboring towns and fairs for entertainment. The fact that he was not working while the other members of the boxing club were gainfully employed created a schism between Branwell and them.

Moreover, Branwell now had to borrow money for sparring gloves and for his drinks and meals at the Black Bull and other hotels. Motivated certainly by his natural inclination to assuage his increasing feelings of inadequacy in any way possible, he increased his alcohol intake excessively. Just as his Angrian heroes had chosen expediency to solve their problems, so he would resort to liquor to forget his own. Moreover, drink not only offered him a sense of liberation from pressing cares, but of companionship—so meaningful to one who had depended heavily on his sisters to fill his lonely world.

For Charlotte, Emily, and Anne, who had not even the money to spend for a postage stamp, Branwell's lavish spending was anathema. Neither remonstrances nor reasonable explanations of why he should not indulge in such a life-style stopped Branwell. There was only one way that the bills could be met: Charlotte, who had made up with Miss Wooler, would have to return to Roe Head to teach.

Reverend Branwell was now anxious to carve out a suitable career for his son. The multifaceted Branwell had been enthralled by a variety of possible paths leading, hopefully, to a profession. Convinced, at least outwardly, that he could excel in almost anything he undertook, he looked on a career in music as a distinct possibility in 1834. His favorite composers—Handel, Haydn, and Mozart—and "Sacred Oratorios" would send Branwell into moods of rapture and virtual ecstasy. That his father provided the funds for Branwell's flute and organ lessons, as he had for his daughters' piano lessons, was perfectly natural for a man who valued learning and accomplishments. Branwell achieved the great honor of performing on several occasions at Reverend Brontë's church. As soon as his first enthusiasm for performance waned, his family realized that he was no musical genius. Of the Brontës, Emily alone achieved virtually professional status as a pianist.

Another possible vocation for Branwell had to be found. Art instruction had been imparted to the Brontë children from an early age, and they used to spend hours copying drawings and paintings of such well-known illustrators as William Gilpin, John Henry Fuseli (known for his illustrations of the *Iliad,* the *Odyssey,* and *Paradise Lost*), and John Martin's apocalyptic engravings that hung on the walls of the parsonage. Their acumen in this domain was impressive:

They would take and analyze any print or drawing which came their way, and find out how much thought had gone to its composition, what ideas it was intended to suggest, and what it *did* suggest. In the same spirit, they laboured to design imaginations of their own; they lacked the power of execution, not of conception. At one time, Charlotte had the notion of making her living as an artist, and wearied her eyes in drawing with the pre-Raphaelite minuteness, but not with the pre-Raphaelite accuracy, for she drew from fancy rather than from nature.[17]

As illustrators, Branwell and Charlotte were considered the most talented of the four.

As part of Reverend Brontë's educational plan, he took his children to the "Annual Exhibition of the Northern Society for the Encouragement of the Fine Arts" at Leeds in 1834. The works of the sculptor Joseph Leyland and the portraits of William Robinson were particularly inspirational.

Robinson was engaged to teach painting to the Brontë children. There was no doubt in Reverend Brontë's mind or that of his daughters that Branwell would achieve the status of a professional in short order. After all, had he not painted an oil of himself standing behind his seated sisters? During the painting process, however, he decided to blot himself out. The canvas was described as follows by Mrs. Gaskell:

Charlotte stood, in the womanly dress of that day of jigot sleeves and large collars. On the deeply shadowed side, was Emily, and Anne's gentle face resting on her shoulder. Emily's countenance struck me as full of power; Charlotte's of solicitude; Anne's of tenderness. The two younger seemed hardly to have attained their full growth, though Emily was taller than Charlotte; they had cropped hair, and a more girlish dress. I remember looking on those two sad, earnest, shadowed faces, and wondering whether I could trace the mysterious expression which is said to foretell an early death.[18]

Mrs. Gaskell denigrated the painting: it was "a rough, common-looking oil-painting ... not much better than sign-painting, as to manipulation." Discerning critics, such as Francis A. Leyland, considered Branwell's forms crudely delineated, his colorations uninspiring. In his judgment, he would never be great, but perhaps with study and discipline, he might achieve a modicum of success as a draughtsman.

The question remained as to whether Branwell would have the stamina and perserverance necessary to adhere to the rigorous training required for an artist. Branwell's father and teacher must have deemed such continuous study unnecessary since the potential painter was encouraged to seek admission to the Royal Academy of Arts in London. Financed by family and friends, Branwell left for the capital in 1835. His hopes, at least outwardly, were high. Was it out of fear of failure? and of disappointing his family? Or was it out of apathy? or indulgence in drink? Whatever the reason, once in London Branwell failed to apply or even make an appearance at the Academy schools. Instead, he saw the sights of London during his seven-day stay and seemingly enjoyed the thrill of seeing in real life the places about which he had read so extensively.

That Branwell never brought himself to fulfill his mission must have been a source of deep disappointment and humiliation to him and to his family. Back at Haworth, instead of being dissuaded from opening a studio of portraiture in Bradford, he was encouraged to do just that by his adoring father, family, and friends. Had they reasoned through the situation, they might have asked themselves how a newcomer in art, without sufficient training, could possibly compete with well-established portraitists. The answer was that he could not, and he failed to make a go of his studio work. Hypersensitive, narcissistic, and poor, Branwell once again took the easy way out: wallowing in despair, never having the wisdom or courage to make the necessary effort to succeed in seeing things through to the end, weak, unable to face his family, he added drugs—opium—to his alcoholism.

Branwell was now leading a double life: adjoining lying and deception to his roster of "sins," he succeeded in playing the role of dutiful son when it pleased him to do so, while indulging his bent for alcohol and drugs at other moments. Having accepted his father's invitation to teach at the local Sunday school, Branwell revealed his uncontrollable temper as well as his impatience with the students.

Only by writing about his swashbuckling heroes and their Byronic feats and defeats did Branwell gain release from ever heavier psychological burdens. Still intent upon becoming a writer and deciding it was time for him to seek publication, he wrote to the editor of *Blackwood's Magazine* and, later, to Wordsworth, including samples of his works and asking for their opinions concerning his talent that he knew *had* to be favorable. That no response was forthcoming added to Branwell's sense of hopelessness and moroseness.

Despite deep anguish at the sight of their brother's progressive deterioration, the sisters pursued their writing. Charlotte was intent upon asking Robert Southey, an established poet whom she admired, for his reactions to some of her verses. Unlike Branwell's pompous and arrogant letters, Charlotte's missive was humble. After a two-and-a-half month wait, Southey's reply arrived in March 1837. Conceding her gift for the "faculty of verse," he greatly discouraged her from harboring any thought of earning a livelihood from writing, adding that an attempt to gain "celebrity" as an author is perverse.

Literature cannot be the business of a woman's life, and it ought not to be. The more she is engaged in her proper duties, the less leisure will she have for it, even as an accomplishment and a recreation. To those duties you have not yet been called, and when you are you will be less eager for celebrity.[19]

He further admonished her about the dangers of heightened imagination and daydreaming; these, he said, are "likely to induce a distempered state of mind." His negative view of her writing and of her future was not only discouraging, but, perhaps, an articulation of what she feared subliminally and was unable to verbalize. Nevertheless, coupled with feelings of inadequacy were resiliency and a very real faith in her talent as a storyteller. Hadn't she been told time and time again that, when recounting tales to the students of Roe Head, she had terrified them to the point of hysteria with her accounts of ghosts, ghouls, and demons? She also possessed the gift of regaling them with the beautiful intricacies of romance: lovers, separated and brought together by some quirk of fate; or the agony of betrayal after swearing eternal fidelity to one another. Were not Byron and Scott and Gothic novels among her favorites?

Whenever the Brontë sisters were faced with a problem or wished to discuss some point concerning their lives or their writings, they would wait until nine in the evening, after Miss Branwell, their aunt, had gone to bed and they had accomplished whatever duties had been assigned to them. Then, meeting upstairs in their small quarters they "began to pace the room backwards and forwards, up and down," glancing into the firelight for clarification since the candles were extinguished at ten.[20] Their ability to discuss with each other the cares of the day, their future plans, or whatever was in their minds, enabled them to come to grips, at least to a certain extent, with their anxieties.

Charlotte was deeply preoccupied at this point with her future course as a writer. Her creative life seemed to have reached an impasse. Impatience and seeming dissatisfaction with the tales she was writing peppered her thoughts. She knew she *must* write from experience, yet some of the episodes she tried to verbalize were excruciatingly painful, increasing her already powerful inner turmoil. In her novelette, "Stancliffe's Hotel" (1838), her description of an opium addict certainly modeled on her brother left her with a gaping wound.

There was vacancy in his aspect and dreamy stupor. Meantime the ecstatic smiles which had every now and then . . . passed like sunshine over his countenance began to recur with fainter effect and at longer intervals—the almost sensual look of intense gratification and absorption gave place to an air of fatigue.

True to life, but also painful was her cynical, although insightful, "Captain Henry Hastings," also based in part on Branwell's humiliating and depressing condition. Were Charlotte's feelings concerning her brother changing from compassion to disgust? "Captain Henry Hastings" revolves around the life of the once heroic, but now vitiated military man and the role his loyal and devoted sister plays in her fruitless attempt to save him.

Charlotte was becoming increasingly objective and critical in her outlook on life. In "Caroline Vernon," dated 1839, morality—and not merely pathos and drama—becomes an issue. Here, as in the later *Jane Eyre*, she takes a firm stand against the paltry state of probity among French ladies.

Although Charlotte might have wanted to remain at home indefinitely, her sense of obligation, heightened by the family's diminishing financial resources due in part to her brother's increasing debts, prompted her to offer her services as nursery governess to the Sidgwick family of Stonegappe, Lothersdale. She remained, however, for only three months.

Emily, who would also attempt once again to earn her living, accepted a post as teacher at Law Hill School near Halifax, whose larger student body of forty caused her workload to be excessive.

Her duties began at six in the morning, continuing until nearly eleven at night, with but a half hour for exercise. Emily resigned after approximately six months. Despite drudgery and extreme fatigue, however, she wrote around thirty poems during her stay at Law Hill School. At home again, Emily wrote with even greater gusto, completing two-thirds of all of her poetry by 1840.

Compelled now to draw increasingly upon herself and her beloved moors for emotional nourishment, Emily needed new strength to deal with her brother's increasingly deteriorating physical condition, as well as to provide protection for Anne who, in fact, found the new curate, William Weightman, charming and attractive. Because he flirted with Ellen Nussey, Emily needed to set herself up as official watchdog to guard her sister.

Emily did not suffer the religious torment that plagued the lives of her sisters; nor was she morbidly obsessed with notions of sin or guilt. She was relatively at peace with herself. Her intense love for everything that lived in nature kept her spirits and lust for life high, so that some came to call her a pagan. Most especially, she enjoyed the companionship of dogs. Hers, the large and fierce "Keeper" from whom she demanded complete discipline, obeyed no one but Emily, yet had his moments of savagery. For example, Aunt Branwell had extracted the promise from Emily not to let Keeper into the house because he was in the habit of jumping on the beds and soiling the linens. Soon thereafter, upon noticing Keeper on one of the beds, Emily grabbed him and dragged the growling animal down the stairs. Fearing the dog would jump at her throat, but without a stick to beat him, she used her bare fists against his muzzle. Other incidents of this nature revealed Emily's capacity for both love and cruelty. When a strange dog bit her in the street she took a red-hot iron to cauterize the wound, preferring to keep the incident a secret from her family until the incubation period for rabies was over.

Branwell's problems, however, were sapping the vitality of the Brontë family. He drifted from job to job, unable to hold employment for any length of time; his speech took on a coarseness to which the Brontës were unaccustomed. At his father's instigation, he tried several different jobs: a clerk, in charge of the small Leeds-Manchester railroad station; part-time employment as the Haworth's sexton's secretary attending to the commissioning and fashioning of gravestones; tutoring posts. Each attempt at holding down a job ended in failure.

Although the family funds decreased in proportion to Branwell's inceasing debts, their love for this comely but weak lad was
tinged with pity. He was

very handsome; the forehead is massive, the eye well set, and the expression of it fine and intellectual; the nose too is good; but there are coarse
lines about the mouth, and the lips, though of handsome shape, are loose
and thick, indicating self-indulgence, while the slightly retreating chin
conveys an idea of weakness of will. His hair and complexion were
sandy. He had enough of Irish blood in him to make his manners frank
and genial, with a kind of natural gallantry about them.[21]

The Brontë sisters, compelled with urgency to face the reality of
their economic situation, decided that in order to remain solvent
and become financially independent they would have to open a
school. Such a step required an enhancement of their qualifications by improvement of their knowledge of French and German.
To this end, Charlotte and Emily, despite the latter's reclusive
temperament, enrolled in February 1842 at the Pensionnate Héger in Brussels. Meanwhile, Anne remained at home to attend to
the household chores and pursue her writing. Her poems, particularly her Gondal series, were imaginative, even relatively joyful
at times, and strangely uninhibited, revolving as they did around
passionate love situations, nature, religious fervor, and the inevi-
tability of death.

Although considered physically frail, Anne was far from being
either passive or weak, as Charlotte had described her. Her two
posts as governess, which she maintained for nearly five years,
provided opportunity to demonstrate her courage and audacity.
Having been engaged by the Ingham family in 1839 to educate
the two oldest of their five children, she was, much to her dismay,
dismissed for incompetence after two terms. Rather than despair,
she sought another post which she held from 1841 to 1845 as
governess for the Robinson's son and three daughters. Mr. Robinson, an ordained minister who preferred living as a squire on
his estate, and his wife, the daughter of a clergyman and wealthy
in her own right, were far from admirable employers. Anne had
made up her mind, however, to interiorize her anger and restrain
manifestations of her disgust for their hypocritical and deceitful
comportment, and for their exploitation of those in their service.
Feelings of estrangement and loneliness, coupled with a sense of

degradation, were expressed openly in Anne's letters to her family and in her "diary paper" (a sealed square folded into four parts, to be opened four years later). "I dislike my situation and wish to change it," she wrote on July 30, 1841. A month later, on July 31, 1845, Anne noted: "and if I had known that I had four years longer to stay how wretched I should have been; but during my stay I have had some very unpleasant and undreamt-of experiences of human nature."[22]

Anne had learned a great deal from the fiasco of her first post. Her behavior patterns had to change if she were to succeed as a governess; she would have to dominate her emotions, hold her feelings in check, and allow reason to prevail at all times. It is believed that it was at this time that Anne fell in love with her father's handsome curate, William Weightman, the very one from whom Emily tried to protect her. Whether Weightman had or had not an eye for the ladies, as Charlotte's letter to Ellen Nussey suggests, or whether he loved Anne alone, will probably never be known.

He sits opposite to Anne at church sighing softly and looking out of the corners of his eyes to win her attention—and Anne is so quiet, her look so downcast—they are a picture—He would be the better of a comfortable wife like you to settle him, you would settle him I believe—nobody else would.[23]

No marriage, however, was forthcoming, since Weightman died of cholera in the autumn of 1841, while Anne was still at the Robinsons'.

Meanwhile, Branwell's life was becoming more chaotic. The greater his sense of failure, the more intolerable grew his presence at home. Rather than take stock of himself, he blamed his family's austere ways and narrow views for his weaknesses. Branwell, the adolescent, found it easier verbally to flagellate others than himself for his own shortcomings. His family reprimanded him as gently as they could, but it was too late to reform what had no contours to begin with. The most harrowing of all of Branwell's experiences of failure was his dismissal by the ailing Mr. Robinson from his post as tutor at Thorp Green, the very post that Anne had obtained for him. He had fallen in love with his employer's wife and even dreamed of marrying her. The relationship, and its disastrous ending for Branwell, was either a figment of his imagination or the result of the heartlessness of a highly sophisticated and immoral woman who thought she would use this vulnerable young man's passion to flatter her own pride. To assuage the sorrow of his rejection, Branwell once again increased his dosages of alcohol and opium.

That Charlotte and Emily, who had never ventured beyond Yorkshire county, departed for the Pensionnat Héger in Brussels, may be viewed as a heroic act for two such shy and retiring women. Emily's adaptation would certainly be far more difficult than Charlotte's, whose experiences away from home, although not always happy, were psychologically beneficial in that they opened her eyes to a variety of behavioral types and patternings. Emily, of all the Brontë sisters, was the most introverted, secretive and perhaps in her own way the most intransigent. Nor had she any friends or need of them, so utterly and irremediably withdrawn was she. Her family, her home, her writing, and the moors were the focus of her life. During the nine months she had spent away from Haworth, either at Roe Head School or teaching at Law Hill School, she had grown deeply homesick. But she was determined to succeed at the Pensionnat Heger.

Accompanied by Reverend Brontë, Emily and Charlotte left for London on February 8, 1842, then sailed to Ostend four days later. As expected, the beginning of the girls' stay in Brussels was difficult. Linguistic, religious, and social barriers, in addition to their withdrawn personalities, isolated them from the other eighty students. Also serving to segregate them from the group was their old-fashioned dress and their different ideas on education. Constantine Héger's rotelike method of instruction particularly displeased Emily, who believed it stifled any and all originality. Héger admired Emily for her extreme self-discipline, perseverance, and imagination. Years later, he described her as follows:

She should have been a man—a great navigator. . . . Her powerful reason would have deduced new spheres of discovery from the knowledge of the old; and her strong, imperious will would never have been daunted by opposition or difficulty; never have given way but with life.[24]

With regard to Charlotte, Mr. Héger said that Emily

appeared egotistical and exacting compared to Charlotte, who was always unselfish . . . and in the anxiety of the elder to make her younger sister contented, she allowed her to exercise a kind of unconscious tyranny over her.[25]

The Brontës were not totally alone in Brussels. Charlotte's friends the Taylors, who lived outside the city, invited them to their home, as did their cousins, the Jenkins, who resided in the metropolis. Mrs. Jenkins said years later that she used to ask Charlotte and Emily

to spend Sundays and holidays with her, until she found that they felt more pain than pleasure from such visits. Emily hardly ever uttered more than a monosyllable. Charlotte was sometimes excited sufficiently to speak eloquently and well—on certain subjects; but before her tongue was thus loosened, she had a habit of gardually wheeling round on her chair, so as almost to conceal her face from the person to whom she was speaking.[26]

Although the Brontës' shyness and isolation eased somewhat during their stay at the Pensionnat Héger, their far from dazzling opinion of the student body did not alter. Charlotte wrote:

If the national character of the Belgians is to be measured by the character of most of the girls in this school, it is a character singularly cold, selfish, animal, and inferior. They are very mutinous and difficult for the teachers to manage; and their principles are rotten to the core. We avoid them, which it is not difficult to do, as we have the brand of Protestantism and Anglicism upon us.[27]

Nor was she less outspoken concerning her distaste for Roman Catholicism.

People talk of the danger which Protestants expose themselves to, in going to reside in Catholic countries, and thereby running the chance of changing their faith. My advice to all Protestants who are tempted to do anything so besotted as turn Catholic is, to walk over the sea on to the Continent; to attend mass sedulously for a time; to note well the mummeries thereof; also the idiotic, mercenary aspect of all the priests; and *then,* if they are still disposed to consider Papistry in any other light than a most feeble, childish piece of humbug, let them turn Papist at once—that's all. I consider Methodism, Quakerism, and the extremes of High and Low Churchism foolish, but Roman Catholicism beats them all. At the same time, allow me to tell you, that there are some Catholics who are as good as any Christians can be to whom the Bible is a sealed book, and much better than many Protestants.[28]

When the school term ended in July, the Hégers, impressed by the sisters' diligence and intellectual superiority, asked them to return after their vacation under different terms. Instead of paying tuition, Emily, now an accomplished pianist, would earn a modest sum teaching music, and Charlotte, English. In November, however, when Miss Branwell, the Brontës' aunt, suffered her fatal illness, the sisters were called home. Frugal always, she left the much-surprised sisters 350 pounds each. Branwell, whom she believed to be a genius, was given nothing since he would be a good earner.

Emily's unhappiness away from home, as well as the security yielded to her by her small inheritance, helped her to decide not to return to the Pensionnat Héger in January 1843. Moreover, someone had to remain home with their father and brother. It was at this period Reverend Brontë allegedly taught Emily to fire a gun and, seemingly, she became an expert shot. Her concern for Branwell alone intruded upon the joy experienced roaming the moors, observing the cloud formations, the sprouting flowers in springtime, and the cleansing winds. His alcoholism, drug addiction, and self-indulgence, had become aggravated.

Charlotte opted to return to Brussels, and there to live out one of the most conflicted and hurtful events of her life. She fell in love with her mentor, Constantine Héger, a family man and devout Catholic. Misinterpreting as passion the vigor he expended teaching her privately, her Byronic emotions swelled uncontrolled. Fortunately, her Christian upbringing and her terror of sin held her cascading sexual fantasies in check. Wives frequently sense emotional upheavals in those with whom their husbands enjoy close proximity. Mrs. Héger, discerning the extent of Charlotte's attachment to her husband, grew cold and distant, thus increasing Charlotte's already important sense of isolation. Distrustful of everyone except for her beloved Mr. Héger, in whose kind heart she had faith, her feelings of alienation grew particularly acute during the five-week vacation period, when she was left alone in the dormitory. To her friend, Ellen Nussey, Charlotte wrote: "I am in low spirits, and that earth and heaven are dreary and empty to me at this moment." Evidence of her impatience to return to the parsonage with the new year is implicit in her letter to Emily. "Low spirits have afflicted me much lately, but I hope all will be well when I get home . . . I am not ill in body. It is only the mind which is a trifle shaken—for want of comfort."[29] Unable to bear the sorrow and suffering resulting from her unrequited love for Mr. Héger, although she believed in his affection for her, Charlotte resigned her position and left for Haworth on January 1, 1844.

Upon her return to the parsonage, she and her sisters entertained hopes of founding a school: "The Misses Brontë's Establishment for the Board of Education of a limited number of young ladies [at] the Parsonage, Haworth." Disappointment also in this domain faced them, for not one application was received. Moreover, Reverend Brontë's health was a source for worry: his cataracts and increasing blindness necessitated an operation. Branwell's rapidly deteriorating physical condition completed the sense of failure that blanketed the atmosphere.

What kept Charlotte intact were the confessional letters she wrote to Mr. Héger, in which she revealed her sorrow, her very real fear of blindness, and the meaningfulness of his missives to her.

Formerly I passed whole days and weeks and months in writing, not wholly without result, for Southey and Coleridge—two of our best authors, to whom I sent certain manuscripts—were good enough to express their approval; but now my sight is too weak to write. Were I to write much I should become blind. This weakness of sight is a terrible hindrance to me. Otherwise do you know what I should do, Monsieur? I should write a book, and I should dedicate it to my literature master—to the only master I ever had—to you, Monsieur. I have often told you in French how much I respect you—how much I am indebted to your goodness, to your advice; I should like to say it once in English. But that cannot be—it is not to be thought of.[30]

That Charlotte received only one letter from Mr. Héger obliged her to face facts and no longer allow herself the luxury of waxing adolescence as when writing her Angrian love-adventures. Because she had lived and breathed a *real* passion for the first time in her life, and not merely modeled her feelings on borrowings from Byron and Coleridge, her prose would take on a corrosive and painful authenticity. Her poetry, however, would remain confessional and passionate, bathing in a world of make-believe:

> He saw my heart's woe, discerned my soul's anguish;
> How in fever, in thirst, in atrophy it pined;
> Knew he could heal, yet looked and let it languish,
> To its moans spirit-deaf, to its pangs spirit-blind. . . .
>
> In dark remorse I rose—I rose in darker shame,
> Self-condemned I withdrew to an exile from my kind;

> A solitude I sought where mortal never came,
> Hoping in its wilds forgetfulness to find.

Although Emily had not experienced Charlotte's love crisis, she felt the time propitious to put together a secret project of her own. In February 1844, she divided the poems she had written throughout the years in two notebooks. The first, entitled "Gondal Poems," included forty-five poems; the second, untitled, thirty-one. Quite by chance, Charlotte found Emily's poetry lying on a table and read it. Her reaction was traumatic.

Something more than surprise seized me,—a deep conviction that these were not common effusions, or at all like the poetry women generally write. I thought them condensed and terse, vigorous and genuine. To my ear, they had also a peculiar music—wild, melancholy, and elevating.[31]

When Emily learned that Charlotte had read her poems, she was furious. Had she wanted to hide from her sisters her preoccupation with love, treachery, alienation, and, most obsessively, with death? Some of her Gondal ballads would certainly reveal what she sought to keep mute: her death-oriented world. Was her description of the slaying of the Roman Emperor King Julius, in the following poem, a premonitory vision of her own demise?

> That death he took a certain aim,
> For Death is stony-hearted
> And in the Zenith of his fame
> Both power and life departed.

Or were the lamentations of Julius's beloved, fifteen years after his demise, paradigmatic of Emily's own longing to depart from this life—a vale of tears for her?

> Cold in the earth, and the deep snow piled above thee!
> Far, far removed, cold in the dreary grave!
> Have I forgot, my Only Love, to love thee,
> Severed at last by Time's all-wearing wave?

When Emily's anger finally subsided, Anne confessed to her sisters that she, too, had been writing poems in secret. The sisters then decided to use thirty-five pounds of their inheritance to publish a volume of their verses. Because of Emily's insistence upon utter secrecy, and because of society's condescending attitude toward women writers, they used the pseudonyms of Currer, Ellis, and Acton Bell. Their first works, *Poems by Currer, Ellis, and Acton Bell,* published by Aylott and Jones, appeared in May 1846.

Despite several favorable reviews, fame was not yet to come to the Brontë sisters. That only two copies of their *Poems* were sold by July did not discourage them from setting to work almost immediately on novels: Charlotte, *The Professor;* Emily, *Wuthering Heights;* and Anne, *Agnes Grey.* Once the daily chores were completed, the sisters would retire to their small sitting room and discuss the progress of their fiction, each one reading the other's work. Once completed, they made up a list of publishers to whom they would send their novels, suffering week after week the deep distress of rejection. Finally, by July 1847, Thomas Cautley Newby accepted *Wuthering Heights* and *Agnes Grey,* but not *The Professor.* Although it was stipulated that neither Emily nor Anne would have to assume publication costs, they would, nevertheless, be obliged to advance fifty pounds against the sale of 250 copies.

Charlotte met adversity head-on and decided that rather than despair over the rejection of *The Professor,* she would begin another work. The opportunity to do so was offered her when she took the nearly blind reverend to Manchester for a cataract operation. She began *Jane Eyre* during her stay in the boardinghouse while she was ministering postoperative care to her father. Unlike *The Professor,* in which she had purposefully toned down her imagination and poetic bent, she would let these flow forth easily, tempered only by reasoned thought and a tightly structured plot line. When, in August 1847, she sent the completed manuscript to Smith, Elder and Company, it was accepted almost immediately.

Not only was Currer Bell's *Jane Eyre,* which appeared on October 16, 1847, lauded by the critics, but its author received five hundred pounds from her publisher. Hopes for further successes were no longer a dream. Emily and Anne also benefited from Charlotte's incredible rise to fame. When their publisher, Cautley Newby, who had held off publishing *Wuthering Heights* and *Agnes Grey,* read the outstanding reviews in praise of *Jane Eyre,* Ellis Bell's *Wuthering Heights* and Acton Bell's *Agnes Grey* were brought out almost immediately. The criticisms Anne received were not always praiseworthy: some reviewers accused her of "exaggeration" and of belaboring the painful lot of the governess. Others, however, praised her for her acute powers of observation.

Despite some favorable reviews of *Wuthering Heights,* most critics misunderstood Emily's literary endeavor, sidestepping its real meaning. The fifty pounds advanced to the publisher were never refunded to Emily or Anne.

After the publication of *Wuthering Heights,* Emily withdrew increasingly into her own world. Dissension between the two older sisters erupted after Charlotte and Anne, having been taken as a single person by several critics, went to London to prove the separate identities of the Bells to their publisher. Charlotte confessed that during her London stay "I committed a grand error in betraying his [Ellis's] identity to you and Mr. Smith. It was inadvertent—the words 'we are three sisters' escaped me before I was aware.... I regret it bitterly now, for I find it is against every feeling and intention of Ellis Bell."[32] Either unforgiving, or suffering a mental breakdown, Emily never wrote again.

Meanwhile, Anne, still working as a governess for the Robinsons and thinking her brother would be an ideal tutor for her employer's son, suggested they employ him, which they did. Things, as already noted, did not work out well. Branwell fell in love with the attractive and flirtatious Mrs. Robinson, seventeen years his senior. Anne, unable to reason with her brother, conveying her reactions in her poem, "If This Be All":

> Grieving to look on vice and sin,
> Yet powerless to quell,
> The silent current from within,
> The outward torrent's swell.

Devastated by his dismissal, Branwell lamented his sorrow in a letter to a friend:

I have lain during nine long weeks utterly shattered in body and broken down in mind. The probability of her [Mrs. Robinson] becoming free to give me herself and estate never rose to drive away the prospect of her decline under her present grief. I dread, too, the wreck of my mind and body, which God knows during a short life have been severely tried. Eleven continuous nights of sleepless horror reduced me almost to blindness, and being taken into Wales to recover, the sweet scenery, the sea, the sound of music caused me fits of unspeakable distress.[33]

After Mr. Robinson's death, Mrs. Robinson, upon the advice of her attorneys, sent her coachman to the Black Bull Hotel to tell Branwell that her husband had written a codicil to his will stating that, should his wife see Branwell again, she would not only be completely disinherited, but would not be allowed the care of their children. Naïve as always, and believing her to be in a state of mad grief at the thought of not being able to see him, he accepted the interdict with deep sorrow. The truth of the matter was that the materialistic and clever Mrs. Robinson was in the process of arranging a lucrative marriage for herself, with Sir Edward Scott, whose wife was expected to die shortly. When Branwell heard of the couple's marriage on November 8, 1848, he was distraught. His alcoholism and drug addiction grew steadily worse, compensatory for his feelings of devastation and bereavement. More and more he dwelled upon the past, his childhood, continued to mourn the death of his beloved sister Maria, and yearned for his own demise. Dominant as well in this narcissistic young man was his terror of physical decay.

I dread a single hint at physical decay as the criminal does each tick of the clock which must toll his knell. When this firm foot can no longer tread the heather, this warm blood no longer thrill to a woman's touch, this working brain no longer teem with thick-coming fancies, this omnivorous stomach no longer bear its three bottles or twenty tumblers—then what the devil is Alexander Percy to do!... I am not a woman to bear pains with patience so the life of an invalid would kill me or drive me mad.[34]

Branwell was heavily in debt, obtaining credit from anyone he could, including the landlord of one of his haunts, the Old Cock at Halifax. The Brontës had to suffer yet another humiliation—a summons brought by the sheriff. Pooling their resources, Branwell's sisters paid part of the debt owed by their brother. Anger at their brother's idleness, weakness, and helplessness was compounded by their anguish and pain at the very real possibility of losing him.

Branwell's physical and psychological deterioration had already taken its toll. Skeletal because of loss of appetite, unable to sleep by night, he spent the daylight hours in bed, occasionally perusing a copy of *Blackwood's Magazine,* which he had so enjoyed as a child. One evening he fell asleep in bed, neglecting to blow out his candle. Anne, who went to look in on him, found his bed curtains aflame. Hysterical with fright and not strong enough to lift the stupefied Branwell from his bed, she called to Emily, whose presence of mind was astounding. Armed with buckets of water from the kitchen, she lifted her insensible brother's sleeping form onto the floor, after which she pulled down the bed curtains and poured water over them. Her single directive to her sister was: "Don't tell Papa."[35]

Because the family feared Branwell might commit suicide, Reverend Brontë decided to have him share his room with him, as in his childhood. But the father accepted his son's destiny, as night after night he listened to his mournful hallucinations, which were interspersed with moments of lucidity. On Sunday morning, September 24, 1848, as the family was preparing to go to church, Branwell's childhood friend, John Brown, went up to his room to keep him company. Suddenly, Branwell grabbed his hand and cried out: "Oh, John, I'm dying!" after which, Branwell slipped out of reach.[36]

The family grieved. Charlotte, suffering severely from headache, dizziness, internal pain, biliousness, and fever, was unable to attend her brother's funeral. Emily, perhaps closest to Branwell and the one to suffer most deeply throughout his long illness, was present at the funeral. It was on that chill and drizzly day that Emily caught the cold that rapidly turned into galloping consumption. Insurmountable suffering marked Charlotte as she watched her sister's decline:

Never in all her life had she lingered over any task that lay before her, and she did not linger now. She sank rapidly. She made haste to leave us. . . . Day by day, when I saw with what a front she met suffering, I looked on her with an anguish of wonder and love. I have seen nothing like it; but, indeed, I have never seen her parallel in anything. Stronger than a man, simpler than a child, her nature stood alone. The awful point was that, while full of ruth for others, on herself she had no pity; the spirit was inexorable to the flesh; from the trembling hands, the unnerved limbs, the fading eyes, the same service was exacted as they had rendered in health. To stand by and witness this, and not dare to remonstrate, was a pain no words can render.[37]

Aware perhaps of the futility of medical aid, or secretly motivated by a death wish, Emily refused to see a doctor or take any medicines; nor did she remain in bed, although she grew weaker daily. While sewing in a desultory fashion in the parlor, on December 19, she told her sisters that if they wanted to send for a doctor she would be willing to see one. She died two hours later.

Had Emily, like her brother, also longed for death, as the following poem suggests?

> Dead, dead is my joy,
> I long to be at rest;
> I wish the damp earth covered
> This desolate breast.

Charlotte was deeply traumatized by Emily's demise, but more fulgurating torment was to follow. Anne, the last of her cherished sisters, and always fragile, began suffering pain in her arm, fevers in the afternoon and evening, cough, loss of appetite, and grew frighteningly thin and weak. Her will to live had all but vanished. When the doctor was called in January, his prognosis was devastating. Charlotte, forced to carry on despite her sorrow, heard her father's admonition: "Charlotte, you must bear up—I shall sink if you fail me." As a last resort and hoping for a miracle, she and her friend took Anne to Scarborough, which she had so wanted to visit again.

[Anne's] decline is gradual and fluctuating; but its nature is not doubtful. . . . In spirit she is resigned: at heart she is—I believe—a true Christian. She looks beyond this life—and regards her Home and Rest as elsewhere than on Earth. May God support her and all of us through the trial of lingering sickness, and aid her in the last hour when the struggle which separates soul from body must be gone through.[38]

On the morning of May 28, 1849, the deeply religious Anne waited patiently and serenely for death.

> I felt that my Redeemer lived,
> I did not fear to die;
> I felt that I should rise again
> To immortality.

The wistul Anne's departure left Charlotte alone with her father in the bleakest of houses and surroundings. From their windows they looked down upon the graves of all those whom they had loved. Charlotte could muster up only one antidote to her numbing pain: writing. During the long months preceding and after her sisters' deaths, she worked on another novel, *Shirley* (1849), which she dedicated to William Makepeace Thackeray. Although not earning the success of her *Jane Eyre*, it was, nevertheless, well received. When her readers finally discovered that the now-renowned author was not a man, but a spinster from

Yorkshire, whose knowledge of passion and love rang so true, they were intrigued. Invited to London, adulated on all sides, the still painfully shy writer enjoyed as best she could the little happiness awarded her.

Emotionally drained upon her return to the parsonage, Charlotte found her bereavement growing rather than diminishing. Her aging father, more and more demanding of her time and company, increased the aching void she felt in her heart. Without her sisters as confidantes she opened her heart to Ellen Nussey.

My reserve, however, has its foundation not in design, but in necessity—I am silent because I have literally *nothing to say.* I might indeed repeat over and over again that my life is a pale blank and often a very weary burden—and that the Future sometimes appals me—but what end could be answered by such repetition except to weary you and enervate myself?

The evils that now and then wring a groan from my heart—lie in position—not that I am a *single* woman and likely to remain a *single* woman—but because I am a *lonely* woman and likely to be *lonely.* But it cannot be helped and therefore *imperatively must be borne*—and borne too with as few words about it as may be.[39]

The still-smarting Charlotte decided it was time to write about her Belgian experience and get it out of her system. She had only alluded to her traumatic experience in her previous works, but had never really grappled with the hurt. Even after the publication of *Villette* (1853), Charlotte's utter dejection was not mitigated by generally favorably reviews.

Charlotte needed and wanted change. When she received an unexpected proposal of marriage from Reverend Brontë's curate, Arthur Bell Nicholls, in the spring of 1853, she would have accepted it had her father not been enraged by the thought that his daughter would be taken away from him. When Nicholls resigned his post after the dutiful Charlotte refused to marry him, her dilemma became all the more acute: she would either break Nicholls's heart or disobey her father.

What prevented Charlotte from marrying Nicholls was the fact that she did not love him. Nor years back had she loved Henry Nussey, Ellen's brother, who proposed to her in 1838. Only one man had stirred her heart, Mr. Constantine Héger; he was the only one for whom she would be willing to die.

> For me the universe is dumb,
> Stone-deaf, and blank, and wholly blind;

> Life I must bound, existence sum
> In the strait limits of one mind;
>
> That mind my own. Oh! narrow cell;
> Dark—imageless—a living tomb!
> There must I sleep, there wake and dwell
> Content, with palsy, pain, and gloom.

No longer young, Charlotte finally realized that understanding and kindness, rather than intense passion, might yield her greater joy at this time in her life. Nicholls, who loved Charlotte deeply, continued to court her despite her refusals and finally, perhaps out of pity for him or simply not wishing to spend the rest of her life in solitude, they married on June 29, 1854.

Returning to Haworth with Reverend Brontë's permission, Charlotte became the lady of the house for husband and father. Such a role must have brought her fulfillment for she no longer felt compelled to write. Or, perhaps she had nothing more to say about herself and her world. The contentment and pleasure that filled her days, however, were of short duration. Her pregnancy might have drained her energies, accounting for her weakened health and the cold she caught when strolling with her husband toward the waterfall on the moors. She, like her sisters, was also plagued by consumption, a disease that carried away countless people in nineteenth-century Europe. Despite her husband's fervent prayers and her own certainty of recovering, she died on March 31, 1855.

The poem Charlotte wrote "On the Death of Anne Brontë" perhaps best conveys her own feelings of immeasurable affliction that nothing earthly could alleviate:

> There's little joy in life for me,
>   And little terror in the grave;
> I've lived the parting hour to see
>   Of one I would have died to save. . . .
>
> Although I knew that we had lost
>   The hope and glory of our life;
> And now, benighted, tempest-tossed,
>   Must bear alone the weary strife.

Part II

The Works

2

Patrick Branwell Brontë: Eternal Adolescent

> There was a light—but it is gone.
> There was a Hope—but all is o'er,
> And friendless, sightless, left alone,
> I go where thou hast gone before,
> And yet I shall not see thee more.
> Ha! say not that the dying man
> Can only think of present pain,
> Oh no! Oh no! it is not so,
> For where, Maria, where art THOU![1]

Branwell, like Romantics such as Byron, Shelley, and Coleridge, cultivated his imagination and emotions rather than his reason, thereby yielding to the continuous lure and excitement of the adventuresome, supernatural, morbid, and melancholy in life. His poetry, prose, and life-style reveal a painful egocentricity and overwhelming tendency toward self-indulgence. Unlike his highly disciplined sisters, who were continually attempting to deal with problems at hand, Branwell spent his time looking back, mournfully, toward his childhood. He set out to recapture and integrate into his present those happy years, through the medium of writing. Because he never had the strength or willpower necessary to step out from the binding and sweetly endearing effects of his childhood, he never grew, psychologically or aesthetically.

Hypersensitive, physically small, and emotionally frail, Branwell, unable to discover his ground bed, may be identified with the *eternal adolescent* type. His weakly structured ego and his highly active imagination were always surging forth uncontrolled, without direction or self-discipline. Moody and frequently subject to an overwhelming sense of despair and helplessness, Branwell always alternated between what Goethe depicted in *The Sufferings of Young Werther* and *Faust* as the heights of jubilation and the depths of despair. Nor did Branwell have the stamina to pursue a professional goal: enthusiastic and self-confident at first, the incipient writer, painter, railroad clerk, organist, tutor, would with time, feel increasingly disappointed with his endeavors, after which lethargy would set in. His lack of success may be attributed to his inability to work regularly, assiduously, or to follow through in pursuit of a chosen goal. Never had he developed the willpower or self-control to perfect his art. Rather than dealing directly with the problems at hand, or even learning to face himself and struggle through whatever the difficulties involved, he sought facile answers in a world of dream and fantasy. Unendowed with genius, unguided by a rigorous and knowledgeable hand, such an individual is most frequently doomed to failure.

Deprivation of a mother figure or *anima* (soul), defined as the unconscious feminine aspect of a man's personality, left Branwell unable to develop a conscious attitude toward woman. In that his projection onto women remained inchoate, he was unequal to the task of differentiating or evaluating the various facets of their personalities. Unless brought into consciousness, the anima is unable to fulfill its function as mediator between the rational and subliminal factors of a personality. The retaining wall that helps prevent subliminal contents from spilling over onto the rational world is nonexistent, and may overwhelm the individual.

Anima images, appearing in creative works, dreams, myths, and legends since time immemorial, range from harlot to the hyperdulian Mary. They are associated with *eros*—that is, with love and relatedness. That Branwell had been divested of his anima—an *eros* figure that establishes feeling relationships in a person's life—indicated that whatever values he saw in women, existed on a most primitive and rudimentary level. A person divested of the ability of differentiating between the multiple facets of a personality, including his own, is given to irrational or instinctual behavior, dominated by the passion of the moment. Branwell's family and friends commented on the fact that throughout his life he was a prey to irresponsible behavior, a victim of his desires, and driven by a sense of urgency. Had his anima been sentient and differentiated, he would have had the power to think out or assess his own personality traits and those of others. His anima would not only have been a source of inspiration to him, but would have led to greater understanding vis-à-vis others, thus opening the door to deeper layers of his psyche and affording him the possibility of building profounder and long-lived relationships.[2]

Feelings of bereavement for Maria and for the paradisiac world of his childhood left Branwell fundamentally solitary, unable to relate to others except on the most superficial of levels. Nor did he overcome his sense of loss for that composite mother/sister/anima figure that Maria had been for him. Appearing as she does in so many of his poems—"Misery I" (1835), "Misery II" (1836), "Caroline" (1837)—she *is* perfection; transcending the workaday world, she assumes divine status. As a spiritual, comforting, and loving force, she has the power to alleviate any and all sorrow, ushering in moods of sweet serenity.

> And entering—Though a sacred stream
> Of radiance round him fell,
> It could not with its silent beam
> His eager spirit quell....
>
> "Where hath my Gentle Lady gone?
> I do not find her here."

The death of Elizabeth, the second eldest Brontë sister, a little over a month after Branwell's beloved Maria, was yet another break in the link with his heavenly past. When told that his mother, Maria, and Elizabeth had all been called to heaven by "Jesus," he alertly questioned the reasons for Jesus to cause his family and him such pain. Was Jesus displeased with the Brontës? Could they, young and old, be to blame for some evil act or thought?

Death, disease, as well as a sense of irremediable guilt and loss settled over the Brontë home, as noted in the previous chapter, wreaking its savage destruction on Branwell's already-faltering sense of identity and purpose. Although he had grown intellectually and psychologically, his intense sense of divestiture remained constant, as attested to by such verses as "Misery I":

> Over Death's unfathomed sea,
> Dark and dread the waves dividing....
> Shores of life, farewell forever,
> Where thy happiness has lain,
> Lost for ever! Death must sever
> All thy hopes and joys and pain!

Instead of inculcating in Branwell's mind the necessity of structuring his life, his sisters spoiled him. Nothing they did could replace Maria's caring and reassuring manner, and their efforts remained emotionally unsatisfying to Branwell. The well-meaning but overly solicitous family did nothing but increase his willful ways and his uncontrollable temper tantrums.[3]

Favored in all ways, as the only boy, Branwell was given a room to himself with a window looking out on the moors, while his sisters slept in a tiny room on cots, folded by day to give them study space. So precious was he to the Brontë family that he was "Brannii the Genii."

Many questions remain unresolved concerning Branwell's upbringing. Why, for example, did Reverend Brontë not send his son to boarding school, as he had his daughters, insisting, instead, on taking charge of his education at home? Perhaps he believed that only he had the expertise necessary to educate him properly in Latin, Greek, and the classics and, certainly, in matters of religion. Or was the father projecting his own unfulfilled desires onto his son? Reverend Brontë had failed to live out the brilliant career his backers had predicted for him and about which he had dreamed in his youth. The attempt to fit Branwell into a mold could only create a crushing dichotomy between what the young man considered himself to be and the adult he *must* become. He had to shine, to excel, to outdo the others in whatever way he could. He was unconsciously terrified that he might not be able to live up to his father's expectations. Nor was his anxiety alleviated by the stern and religiously oriented atmosphere pervading the Brontë home. The shadow of death, sorrow, and sin exacerbated a pronounced Brontë proclivity: morbidity.

Branwell always tried to please his father in every way by living up to the image he had of him: he studied, obeyed, and seemingly carried out whatever orders were given him in order to feel "safe." Wrestling with conflicted views and feelings, Branwell may have felt it wiser to reveal his *good* side only—those characteristics he knew would not disappoint or anger his father. Early in life he mastered the art of hiding his *evil* or *shadow* side, defined as those factors within a personality that might be considered unacceptable. His dual nature, however, created such acute tension within his psyche that a collision between his rational and conscious side and his chaotic subliminal sphere was inevitable.

Such confrontation ignited the sparks that precede explosion—and the temper tantrum ran its course. Branwell was a victim of his own inability to clarify his frustrations and to bring his needs and fears into the open.

The emotionally disadvantaged Branwell, it may be said, lived a dual life from a very early age: on the one hand, he identified with his father's exalted image of him, on the other, with his own understanding of what he was really like. Such a split prevented him from ever digging into his own ground bed. He felt "rootless," unable to find himself or even develop a sense of identity. Lacking the steadiness that would have helped him find his way and given him a sense of harmony and balance, he became a victim of extremes, his acts taking on impulsive and quixotic qualities. Yearning for attention and admiration from father, sisters, and whoever visited the parsonage, Branwell was always ready to impress people with his fine intellect and his great charm—tactics evidently designed to counteract his inherent timidity and sense of inferiority. Matters were not helped by the fact that he was shorter than most young men, physically delicate, high-strung, with poor eyesight, and probably the butt of ridicule because of his golden-red hair. In one of his semiautobiographical narratives, "Life of Warner Howard Warner" (1838), he describes himself as a "shy-looking little being" who would "upon contradiction or scolding" get violently red, bite his lips "which prognosticated something other than a milk and water man."[4]

Writing was Branwell's outlet. His epics, sagas, essays, dialogues, and poems were products of an active imagination, which he developed to an intensely high degree. Poured into his sagas were all the things he could not express overtly: his affects, instinctual drives, fantasies, dreams, ideas, thoughts and concepts. What he wrote became his reality, his way of adapting to the world.

Revealing patterns are contained in Branwell's juvenilia. That heroes rather than heroines abound in his writings is natural; that conquerors are strong types able to sweep over lands and oceans is also to be expected. The antithesis of their creator, Branwell's soldier-characters succeed in dominating events and people by sheer will, perseverance, and fortitude. Battles are fought rather than peace maintained. Cruelties of the bloodiest kind—relatively common, as in most war games—are unusual in the extremely detailed description of the ferocities involved. Interesting as well is the fact that whenever his heroes are put into inextricable situations, rather than apply reason to ferret out alternative routes to resolve their predicament, Branwell causes them to be killed. His sisters, on the other hand, thought out their heroes' or heroines' moves; thus they frequently were able to rectify unpleasant or dangerous situations rather than always resort to blood and gore. With Branwell, destruction in his writings becomes a way of life for his protagonists.

Branwell's "play" habits were symptomatic of his character. Killing off his heroes instead of expending the energy necessary to *think* of ways of extracting them from their dilemma demanded much less effort on his part than attempting to deal with problems rationally and openly. Unlike his sisters who, during their early teens, similarly spent a good deal of their time living in their imaginary world but also had to tend to household duties, Branwell focused on himself. While the girls learned to deal with the problems of running a home, going to school, and working for strangers, their brother studied, or wrote, or amused himself through imagination.

A psychologically fascinating figure appeared in one of Branwell's lead articles (included in *Magazine,* a creative endeavor he and Charlotte worked on) entitled, "Kairail Fish" (1829). This, an incredible creature of the sea, captured by sailors, measured one hundred feet in length by twenty to thirty feet in width. Its horn, which was hooked at the end, had been cut off by sailors, but grew back within half an hour.[5] Branwell's imaginary monster of the sea is reminiscent of the mythical *hydra of Lerna*—a nine-headed poisonous water snake whose very breath was fatal to anyone approaching it. Unlike Hercules, who overpowered this destructive power thanks to the help of Iolaus, his nephew and also his charioteer, Branwell had neither the strength of the Greek hero nor a relative or friend capable of helping him out of his psychological impasse.

What does Branwell's Kairail Fish suggest psychologically? This impregnable and horrific figure living in the depths of his collective unconscious symbolized a latent but destructive power within him, a killer instinct that emerged not only in his writings but also during his mad tempers in the face of problems or entanglements of the moment.[6] Nor, like Hercules, had he recourse to a wiser person who might have helped him deal with and finally accept this negative shadow element raging within him. Had he done so, he possibly could have integrated it into his whole personality, thus rerouting its raging and energetic power.

Branwell's war fantasies became overt shortly after his father gave him his first set of twelve toy soldiers on his seventh birthday (1824); another twelve two years later; a band of Turkish musicians (1827) and another set of Turkish musicians and a band of Indians (1828). Branwell ushered his toy soldiers into life in his action-packed saga, "The History of the Young Men." In this and other works, he, together with his sisters, conjured imaginary lands, thrilling situations enacted by dukes and ladies, noble explorers, pirates, murderers, and cowards, all of whom made their way around the globe from Africa to India, Europe to the South Pacific.

It will be remembered that Branwell gave one of his second set of soldiers—the "Young Men"—to each of his sisters, that Charlotte named hers "The Duke of Wellington," while her brother chose to name his soldier Napoleon. That Napoleon was Wellington's arch enemy, even in play, may suggest an unconscious rivalry for power between Branwell and Charlotte. Did he fear his sister's domineering manner? Or, perhaps, her alliance with her two sisters against him? Was it the ordered, methodical, and secretive ways of a matriarchate that made him feel inferior to them? Was it rejection that he feared? He knew his sisters to be hard workers, persevering, and accepting of their defects. Had they not been told, when entering Roe Head School, that they had never really learned grammar, knew little geography and were lacking in many other disciplines? Such criticism did not drive them to despair, but rather pointed the way to overcoming their inadequacies through *hard* work. Living a relatively cloistered life and treated as a genius by his family, Branwell himself was never put to the test.

Composing "The History of the Young Men" (1830–31) without Charlotte's collaboration, Branwell signed the work John Bud, Esq., "the greatest prose writer." Such epithets not only fulfilled a need to declare his own worth, but were symptomatic of a rebellious streak in him aimed against sister domination. The action of his narrative, replete with wars, killings, cannibals, devils, and monsters, takes place in the eighteenth century in an African region extending from the Gulf of Guinea northwards, including the "famous" and spectacular Glass Town Harbour (later to be called "Verdopolis").[7] The author notes, "I am the Chief Genius Brannii, with me there are three others"—namely, his three sisters. In his fantasy world, Branwell was the leader of them all, that is, he dominated the group: *man* over woman.

The magazine he started, *Branwell's Blackwood's Magazine,* was modeled after *Blackwood's Magazine,* which he and his sisters read diligently, discussed, and abstracted with gusto. After the first three numbers, however, Charlotte, determined to lead the way, to set the goals and style of the venture, took over its direction, thus ending, as she wrote, the "Rule of Dullness." Branwell, the weaker of the two, yielded to her wishes, as stated in his "Concluding Address" (July 29) to his readers.[8]

What was impressive in *Branwell's Blackwood's Magazine* was his incredible knowledge of the art of magazine writing and editing, as well as his familiarity with French culture and history. His articles covering a variety of subjects, ranged from a "Journal of a Frenchman," "The Swiss Artist," "Review of the Causes of the Late War," "The Bay of Glasstown," to all sorts of poems, paintings, etc.[9]

Many types of hero figures—good and bad—appear in the almost frenetically written pages. One of them, Young Soult, the Rymer, was the son of a real historical figure, a marshal in Napoléon's army who was regarded with such respect by the British that years later, when visiting London during the reign of King Louis Philippe, he was invited by Wellington to Apsley House. Interacting with Charlotte in their military strategies, Branwell sought someone of Wellington's stature, and created Soult's son. Charlotte, describing Branwell's hero in terms of Glass Town literature, underscored the stunning identification between her brother and Young Soult.[10]

Although "Young Soult's Poem" (1829) was conventional in every way, it nevertheless sang his hero's unconsciously inflated feelings of himself. Violence grows to unprecedented heights as Branwell focuses on Young Soult's escapades; evil in all of its forms is forever constellated in scenes of excessive brutality, deception, blood and gore, revealing a very real, but still-unconscious hostility on Branwell's part. Charlotte's sagas, on the other hand—even those written in collaboration with her brother—although replete with iniquities, emphasize what is right and disclose a strong sense of morality in her characters who are sound in feeling, and yielding when need be.[11]

Branwell, who frequently identifies with evil, created several satanic creatures, one of the most vicious being Alexander Percy,

Earl of Northangerland.[12] Like the Kairail Fish, Percy loomed large in Branwell's unconscious, again pointing to the powerfully destructive and unassimilated forces inhabiting his psyche.

Understandably, Branwell's emphasis on the military and all of its paraphernalia was implicit in the atmosphere of his generation. Europe had gone through seismic upheavals—the French Revolution, the Reign of Terror, the Napoleonic wars, the Restoration, and in 1830, yet another, although slight political tremor with the advent of Louis Philippe.

A general letdown followed the tempestuous upheavals on the Continent, paving the way for the onset of a type of lethargy, narcissism, and self-indulgent depressive state that the French labeled *mal du siècle*. François-René de Chateaubriand's literary hero René, who suffered from lethargy, apathy, passivity, and general morbidity was the prototype of scores of young men throughout the nineteenth century. That Chateaubriand's name appears on the title page of "Young Soult" suggests the impact of this egocentric Frenchman's writings on Branwell. We know Branwell had read Chateaubriand's *Travels in Greece and the Holy Land*. If he had not actually read *René* (1805), Branwell most certainly had heard of this work, so instrumental in spreading the virus of depression, melancholia, pessimism, lethargy, and vagueness of soul to so many young people in Europe, including its poets, Lamartine, Alfred de Vigny, Alfred de Musset, and the young Hugo and Goethe. In *René*, Chateaubriand probes the feeling world of an impressionable, highly sensitive young man, given to tears and suffering from ennui. The product of a solitary and joyless upbringing in Brittany, René responded emotionally to its forests, moors, and windswept oceans. His only companion and his great love, the single person with whom until her death he shared his fantasies of traveling to distant lands, was Lucile, his high-strung and unbalanced sister.

Unlike the French writer, Branwell did not probe his inner world, but rather focused on externalities, taking his heroes all over the globe. But whereas Chateaubriand traveled to England and to America, Branwell, until almost nineteen, had gone virtually nowhere. Most importantly, he did not possess Chateaubriand's genius.

Whereas many Romantics attached a whole philosophical dimension to their writings, such as a belief in the goodness of humankind—an aftermath of Jean Jacques Rousseau's cult of the "noble savage"—Branwell's juvenilia and his poetry had no moral thesis. In this regard, they differed as well from the writings of the politically oriented English Romantics.

William Wordsworth crossed the Channel and sided with the French Revolutionists, returning only after his family, dismayed by the excesses of the French proletariat, cut off his allowance. During his stay in France, however, he became cognizant of the meaning of political and mob uproar, as well as the injustices of economic disparity. In *Lyrical Ballads* (1798), written with Coleridge, he stated his beliefs that the lives of the poor and destitute are fitting themes for poetry, and that everyday speech should be used rather than the pompous and conventional language of the classicists. Nature was Wordsworth's catalyst. Since it was animated with an active spirit, it remained his companion throughout his life. Branwell was engaged neither in helping the poor nor in political activity. His juvenilia and poetry are devoid of moral obligations or theories; they merely mirror his mood of the moment, motivated by conquest, or waxing in unutterable melancholia.

Branwell was certainly taken with Wordsworth's emphasis on the feeling world (as implicit in "Lines Written a Few Miles above Tintern Abbey") and his mystic passion for Nature, an ally with which he identifies. Likewise Branwell could relate to the world of the opium-addicted Coleridge who delved into strange supernatural realms. Like Coleridge, Branwell believed in the supremacy of the imagination over that of literary rules. Like Coleridge, he was temperamentally weak and unwilling to struggle over the execution of his poetry, rendering his efforts often problematic.

The fact that the Romantics focused mostly on the individual's subjective reactions to their inner and outer world fed directly into Branwell's own narcissistic nature. Shelley's "Prometheus Unbound" and "Excursion" convey the zest of renewed youth, expectancy, marvel, and an idealism that promised a new way on earth—a pledge of heaven. Keats also took refuge from sordid existence by dreaming of marvels. The ancient world of myth prevailed in "Endymion" and "Hyperion," along with divine forms, beautiful beings, and bountiful nature, with its woodlands and caverns. Like the despairing, somber, violent, voluptuous, passionate, reckless, and rebellious Byron, Branwell looked upon himself as both a victim and hero of destiny. He would have liked to live out his passions and sorrows in a "Childe Harold" of his own manufacture, or in the wild and supernatural motifs of Byron's *Manfred, Cain,* and *Don Juan.* Unlike Byron, Branwell joined neither the fight for the liberation of Greece from Ottoman rule, nor any other movement or struggle.

Branwell was a derivative poet; he was talented, to be sure, but not an innovator. He was a rhymer, as was his hero Percy, an explorer of feelings and a fighter—but on paper. Lacking perseverance, rarely if ever did he probe the world of thought in his writings. His themes, images, and frenetic pulsations, therefore, take on a sameness and a monotony that was, interestingly, implicit in some of Wordsworth's later poems, and not infrequently present in the writings of some Romantics, such as Chatterton, "the neglected genius," and others who were fated to die young.

Branwell's imaginary world expanded and ascended in keeping with his moods. His covering letter when sending his poem, "Misery," to *Blackwood's Magazine* on April 8, 1836, instead of being courteous and humble, was aggressive, almost uncouth, and remained unanswered.[13] Nor did Wordsworth reply to his letter written in a similarly arrogant style, in which he enclosed his poem of desperation, "Still and bright, in twilight shining."[14]

Did the editor of *Blackwood's Magazine* and Wordsworth consider Branwell's pained and seething outpourings merely the work of a banal rhymer? Or were they put off by his gushing language and all the trappings of its Gothicism: the dungeon, the darkened sky, the harsh wind, the ancestral glory, the hopelessness of it all? Branwell's bitterness and inner hurt following Wordsworth's silence was perhaps more devastating than his disappointment over the unresponsiveness of the editor of *Blackwood's Magazine.* Nevertheless, that the eternal adolescent's naïve plea for help remained unanswered did not diminish his productivity, though it did wreak havoc on his feelings of self-worth.

Branwell's energy, nevertheless, remained unabated. From the age of ten to seventeen, he wrote more than thirty volumes of stories, poems, plays, journals, histories, literary criticism, not counting those that have been lost or destroyed. His incredible knowledge of French history and literature was impressive as were the vast amounts of information he had amassed concerning multiple subjects including London's topography. Unconsciously, he pressured himself continuously to live *outside* of the world of reality rather than face it and confront the problems of the adolescent.

Loneliness, after his sisters' departures for school or for their posts, might have been instrumental in encouraging Branwell to join the Haworth boxing club, thus finding the companionship of other young men that had been denied him before. Important to him were the workouts he hoped would strengthen his body, in which he took such pride. After all, he might have reasoned, had not Byron been fascinated with sports? As a member of the Boxing Club, the seat of which was the Black Bull Hotel, Branwell met all sorts of people, including, most probably, some unsavory drinking partners. Naïve, unaccustomed to worldly men, he was influenceable. That he felt different from others and set apart, given his education and breeding, was a source of humiliation for him, increasing his already pronounced sense of alienation. Other reasons for the dichotomy between himself and *others* stemmed from the fact that members of the Boxing Club worked for a living while he did not. Whatever small sums he had were given him by his father and sisters. In time, he grew ashamed of his penury, trying to remedy it as best he could by borrowing from anyone willing to lend him whatever amounts he needed at the moment.

Blind to his son's weaknesses, Reverend Brontë still had hopes he would make something of himself. He encouraged Branwell to develop his musical talents, offering him flute and organ lessons; he also gave him the money to attend concerts at Leeds, Bradford, and Keighley. Branwell was particularly drawn to orchestral performances of oratorios by Handel and Masses by Haydn and Mozart. In keeping with his temperament, he returned home overwhelmed by the magnificence of it all. Under the effects of such highs, Branwell wrote about music, interspersing such sequences amid depictions of wars, banquets, theatrical productions, and other thrilling happenings, as evident in his six-volume *Letters to an Englishman* (1831). Particularly intriguing is an imaginary response to a spectacular musical feat that took place in Africa. The audience numbering five or six million people listen enraptured to the sounds of an orchestra comprising ten thousand performers, and two- or three-hundred instruments.[15]

Although Reverend Brontë in his heart of hearts may never really have considered the possibility of a musical career for his son, he did believe in his talent as a painter and did everything possible to help him achieve success. He was impressed, as well he might have been, with Branwell's gift for drawing. Ever since he was a child he had been illustrating his sagas with depictions ranging from Gothic castles fallen into ruin, thatched cottages, dungeons, intricate and bizarre-looking sequences of pillars and spiral staircases à la Piranesi and Fuseli. Impressed with the engravings of John Martin, always accessible to him since they garnished the Parsonage, he frequently emulated what he considered to be Martin's fascinating ancient colonnades and embattlements. Branwell also responded with passion to the works of two Yorkshire artists, Joseph Bentley Leyland, and the portrait painter William Robinson.

So impressed was Reverend Brontë with his son's seemingly intense desire to become an artist that despite his paltry finances, he had him take lessons with Robinson, known for his paintings of Wellington, the duke of York, Princess Sophia, and more. What neither father nor son took into consideration were the years of rigorous training an artist must put himself through in order to become a master.

Moreover, vast differences exist between painting and drawing. That Branwell excelled in the latter did not necessarily mean that he would in the former. Had Branwell proven himself a painter? Seemingly, in 1834 or 1838, the date is unclear, he painted a group portrait of his sisters, which is reproduced on the dust jacket of this book, probably including himself in the center, later blotting out his figure, substituting a pillar in his stead. Branwell's friend and biographer, Francis Leyland (brother of the sculptor), wrote that "he never had been instructed in the right mode of mixing his pigments, or how to use them when properly prepared. . . . He was, therefore, unable to obtain the necessary flesh tints, which require so much delicacy in handling, or the gradations of light and shade, so requisite in . . . a good portrait."[16] Leyland did praise Branwell's fine draughtsmanship, his ability to capture his subjects' likenesses, and the dexterity with which he placed them on the canvas.

Encouraged by his teacher and his family to seek admission to the Royal Academy of Arts in London, Branwell left for the big city in 1835, with high hopes. Why then did he not follow through? Was it out of fear of being rejected? out of apathy? too much liquor? Whatever the answer, Branwell failed even to apply to the Academy schools. He did go sightseeing during his seven-day stay in London and seemingly enjoyed viewing all the places about which he had read. That he never brought himself to fulfill his mission must have been a source of disappointment and humiliation to him. What could he possibly say to family and friends?[17]

Rather than dissuade Branwell from opening a studio of portraiture in Bradford (1839), his family and friends encouraged him to do just that. Although able to boast of having such well-placed citizens as Mr. and Mrs. Kirby sit for him, competition at the time was fierce. Branwell neither had the training nor the experience, perseverence, or luck to become a painter of renown.

His series of failures dug deep and his emotional wounds and unhealed scars rendered him even more helpless than before. Wallowing in despair, never having the wisdom or the courage to make the necessary effort to see things through to the end, he became more deeply addicted to alcohol and drugs, resorting to deceit and prevarication to hide his increasing feelings of degradation from his family. That he was admitted to the Masonic Lodge of Haworth, January 1, 1836, and appointed secretary to the local Temperance society of which his father was president was another example of Reverend Brontë's blindness when it came to his son; it was also a grotesque travesty of morality. So, too, was the teaching post Branwell obtained, but kept for only a short period at the local Sunday school. His explosive temper and impatience with the young students did not serve to endear him to them.

The greater Branwell's sense of failure in the outside world, the more intolerable grew his life at home. Blaming his family's ascetic and narrow views for his weaknesses could no longer alleviate his progressively sinister situation. A scapegoat is frequently in order when a person is unable to shoulder responsibilities. Branwell's family was eminently well suited for the role: they had never understood his intellectual nor his emotional needs. So acutely wounded had Branwell been that even blaming others for his deficiencies no longer alleviated his hurt. In "O God! While I in Pleasure's Wiles," he yearns for strength, although he is aware that he is slipping ever further into dejection and apathy—into a world of eternal sleep.

The severest blows of them all were yet to come: Branwell's dismissal from his tutoring post at Thorp Green for his alleged romance with his employer's wife, Mrs. Robinson; to be followed by the marriage of the newly widowed Mrs. Robinson. That Branwell believed that the sophisticated Mrs. Robinson was in love with him and would marry him once her husband had died is paradigmatic of his naïveté and vulnerability. One might even question the very reality of Branwell's liaison. Was it, perhaps, a figment of his imagination? So out of touch was Branwell with reality that he might have indulged in wishful thinking. Or could she have played the role of mother figure in his life as Mme. de Renal had for Julien Sorel in Stendhal's *The Red and the Black?*

Branwell's irremediable sorrow drove him further and further into alcoholism, drug addiction, and debt. In imitation, seemingly, of De Quincey, he increased his doses of opium, begun, so it is thought, after his period of dejection following his failure as a painter at Bradford.[18] Had not De Quincey in his *Confessions of an Opium Eater* praised the pleasures to be derived from this drug? The effects of opium lasted eight hours, longer than those of liquor, thus increasing the time one could bask in beatitude. Furthermore, liquor was discernible on the breath while opium was not; opium was cheap and could easily be procured on any druggist's shelf in liquid form (laudanum).

Branwell's last work, which was never completed, "And the Weary Are at Rest" (1845), was a conclusion to his Angrian cycle. As to be expected, it showed neither evolution in his writing style nor depth in his characterizations. The same may be said for "Thorp Green," yet another self-absorbed poem:

> I SIT, this evening, far away
> From all I used to know,
> And nought reminds my soul to-day
> Of happy long ago.

For some time, much to his father's dismay, Branwell claimed to be an unbeliever. According to Charlotte, two days before his end, he seemed to have undergone a spiritual transformation: "all at once he seemed to open his heart to a conviction of the existence and worth" of the religion he had affirmed "he would never believe at all." His frequent appeals to God in some of his last poems, such as "Peaceful Death and Painful Life," seem to confirm Charlotte's affirmation.

> Why dost thou sorrow for the happy dead?
> For if their life be lost, their toils are o'er
> And woe and want shall trouble them no more,

Nor ever slept they in an earthly bed
So sound as now they sleep while, dreamless, laid
In the dark chambers of that unknown shore
Where Night and Silence seal each guarded door.

Branwell's death on September 28, 1848, at the age of thirty-
one, yielded this troubled soul calm and serenity.

3

Anne Brontë: "Smouldering Fire"

I hoped amid the brave and strong
My portioned task might lie,
To toil amid the labouring throng
With purpose keen and high.[1]

This stanza from one of Anne's poems, "A Dreadful Darkness Closes In," sums up her commitment to morality and defense of good over evil. The creation of a work of art was not Anne's goal, though the manner in which she expressed herself and some of her characterizations have turned her novels into semiprecious jewels. In depicting insidious vices that might grip a family—or even the world—Anne sought to warn her readers to take immediate steps to rectify their comportment. Even when death was but a few days away, Anne wrote to a friend that although she had no fear of death, she wanted to live "because I long to do some good in the world before I leave it."[2]

Although Anne's focus on morality was in part a sign of the times, her novels were unlike those of such social realists as Harriet Martineau (*A Manchester Strike* [1832]) or Mrs. Elizabeth Gaskell (*Mary Barton* [1848]). Their writings dealt with labor, industry, trade unionism, starvation, squalor, disease, and the like. Intellectually aware of the plight of the needy, Anne had no first-hand experience of their misery, having lived in Haworth or on large estates for the most part. Moreover, her interests were ideologically oriented. Questions of conscience were uppermost in her mind: domesticity, the rights of working women, and abused wives. Anne sought truth and justice via the medium of the word.[3]

Anne was a feminist in her writings. Her voice was raised against the paltry salaries, poor working conditions, and offensive treatment accorded governesses; against society's denigration of working women; against the legal status of married women who had to give over their dowries and fortunes to their husbands, thereby reducing them to slave status and keeping them virtual prisoners of their own homes. That Anne pleaded for self-fulfillment for women and equality of the sexes was understandable, particularly since she was an author. In the preface to the second edition of *The Tenant of Wildfell Hall* she speaks forthrightly on the subject of equality of the sexes.[4]

Anne's earliest writings took the form of poems. Although ideology and autobiography were in evidence, fantasy and a sense of play, rarely evoked in her novels, were conveyed in her stanzaic patternings.

The Poems: "With Purpose Keen and High"

Traditional in their patterned versification, rhyme, rhythm, and imagery, Anne's poems are controlled, smooth, reserved, and ordered. They frequently give the impression even of being somewhat didactic, but they concealed a psyche in turmoil. Plagued by religious anxiety revolving around sin and salvation, to the point of nearly disbelieving in God, her stanzas are marked with loneliness and fear of damnation.

Anne's earliest "Gondal" poems (1836–40), however, were imaginative, relatively joyful at times, hopeful, and strangely uninhibited. Composed as a kind of continuation of the Gondal game begun in 1831 by Emily, and by Anne at a later date, her poems reveal the ingenuity of a child living in isolation, forced to rely on herself for entertainment and excitement. Endowed with fertile imagination, she took what was offered her and by the wizardry of her mind and senses, transforming peaked mountains, troubled seas, distant lands, and impassable roads into exotic visions and visitations.

In the Gondal myth, with all of its romantic interludes, the heroes and heroines find themselves in dungeons, caves, and castles on Gondal island, located somewhere in the North Pacific. Anne's flights of fantasy and forays into the unknown, wherever Gondal whimsy took her, allowed her unreservedly to express her inmost feelings without fear of recognition. She must have felt that the figures of speech she used—symbols, images, and metaphors conjured by day- or night-dreams—were sufficient to mask her innermost secrets from prying eyes. The relative fearlessness of some of Anne's early "Gondal" poems reveal a certain spontaneity and sense of buoyancy that is muted in later poems.

Love is the motif in Anne's sixty-seven-stanza poem "Alexandria and Zenobia." Neither tempestuous nor an escape from earthly existence, love permits the alloying of fantasy and reality, feeling and thought, outer and inner worlds. Thus does she find a means of experiencing that glorious Edenic oneness a child knows prior to the birth of consciousness.

> Fair was the evening and brightly the sun
>   Was shining on desert and grove,
> Sweet were the breezes and balmy the flowers
> And cloudless the heavens above. (July 1, 1837)

Anne drinks in nature in "Alexandria and Zenobia," inviting light as well as darker groves to enclothe her protagonists, and breezes to swell their joy, revealing a sense of physicality and abandon that was repressed in her later works.

All is not joy in "Alexandria and Zenobia." Although romance prevails and heroes and heroines travel to distant and exotic lands to experience bliss in love and beauty, so too do they suffer. The fair young maiden must return to her Gondal land, and sorrowfully part with her fourteen-year-old "Bold beautiful and bright" Alexander.

The need for physical and spiritual freedom, as opposed to the constrictions imposed upon Anne by her family's devout views and by her asthma and related illnesses, is conveyed metaphorically in "The North Wind," signed Alexandrina Zenobia. Brisk, precise, and rhythmical images of active air currents spell freedom so antithetical to the static imprisoning world of the captive locked in a dungeon, listening attentively to every note and rhythmic pattern enunciated by the gusts and breezes from the outside world: "Now deep and loud it thunders round my cell." The poem replicates a whole network of interacting feelings, thanks to the images and personifications that serve to individualize and concretize what could have remained mere abstraction. Anne reveals in subtle and nuanced ways the extent of her stressful spiritual and intellectual existence. Her passionate need for release, evident in the rhythms and momentum of the gusts whirling about her prison, is answered as the wind, now a cosmic force, bears her thoughts to far-off places, over glens and snowcapped mountains, but also on to the bleak and desolate moors she loves so deeply and knows so well.

The element of "Time" also plays a role in Anne's Gondal poems, as, for example, in "Self-Communion," while taking in "Song" the form of a meditation, Anne's words chant the dangers and conflicts awaiting a wandering soul and then shout out the joy experienced when release from fear is attained. The wildness of the faraway landscape, coupled with a passionate plea for vindication and salvation, injects the author with energy to fight Time, a corrosive and eroding power, thus allaying her anguish, as in the following lines from "Song": "Hunted, oppressed, but ever strong to cope— / With toils, and perils—ever full of hope!"

Other "Gondal" poems are less fanciful: mirroring destructive, chaotic, serene, or harmonious moods of the moment, they reveal an urgency in their motifs. Assailed by religious anxiety, Anne's sense of alienation swells as loneliness, dependency, and feelings of inferiority mount. Nevertheless, solace comes to her in small doses, as in the very *act* of writing—a discipline that allows her to decant her sorrows cerebrally, rather than affectively. When powerful and recurrent feelings of dread risk overwhelming her, the obligatory and governed transmutation of her feelings of terror into the word/sign tempers her affectivity with small draughts of calming spiritual security. Was it not written in the Gospel of John: "In the beginning was the Word, and the Word was with God, and Word was God" (1:1)? Likewise Anne transcribed the tremulous nature of her leaps from corrosive grief at the thought of sin and eternal damnation to ineffable joy at the belief in salvation.

Love as a poetic motif was frequently equated with death. In "Yes, thou art gone and never more," Anne mourned the untimely passing of Reverend Willy Weightman (1842). Her feelings of loss and loneliness in her stanzas reveal the absence of a *comforting* power in her life. Viscerality marks the sensations sweeping over her as she opens "the old church door" and penetrates into God's domain, only to be greeted, shockingly, by "cold damp stone." Rather than raising her gaze to sublime spheres, she lowers it to the grounded slab. The warm and giving "angel fair" who had once and not so long ago "gladdened" her heart she now pictures as a frozen corpse. Although filled with despair, the very recollection of his presence, once a source of solace, again imbues her with consoling thoughts, giving strength to face the gaping maw.

Anne injects feelings of dolefulness, anger, and frustration into such poems as "Verses to a Child" (1838), and in the following

"Dreams" (1845), because she had been denied what she hungered for most in life: marriage and children.

> While on my lonely couch I lie,
> I seldom feel myself alone,
> For fancy fills my dreaming eye
> With scenes of pleasures of its own.

Bereft of a mother's nurturing love, Anne well knew the meaning of a child's thirst for warmth and affection—and her own sense of irremediable loss. As she laments, Anne's thoughts ascend from the fearsome void she knew to idealized regions where serenity, harmony in the heart, and integrity of spirit reign.

When tension grows overly acute, religion does not always come to Anne's aid. Rather, it serves to increase her anguish, as evidenced in her eleven-stanza poem "To Cowper." Although marked by banal rhetorical effects and hyperboles ("floods of silent tears") and simplistic and conventional phrases ("The language of my inmost heart"), this poem, perhaps better than the others, discloses Anne's powerful struggle to reject one of the most harrowing obsessional thoughts to preoccupy the Christian world at the time: that of predestination and the possible unworthiness of even the good to be received into heaven.

The pre-Romantic English poet William Cowper (1731–1800), whose poetics Anne admired, convinced that he had been excluded from salvation, went through protracted periods of despair—"religious mania" or insanity, as such antics are called today. Anne had also been exposed to rigorous Calvinistic religious views by her Aunt Branwell: predestination and the Anglican ideology at the time, of eternal punishment for consciously committed sins, the most evil being the rejection of God. Understandable, then, was Anne's terror when thinking about the very real possibility of damnation, and being cast into cauldrons of burning flames. Cowper's words—his "manly rough line"—impacted on her deeply. Is it any wonder that anxiety wrought havoc upon her outlook and sensibilities, as exemplified in such haunting refrains as "*My* sins, *my* sorrows, hopes and fears"? Never before had she been cognizant of the extent of Cowper's horrific "nights of gloom," his "days of misery, / The long long years of dark despair / That crushed and tortured thee." Unlike Cowper, however, Anne struggled to maintain her belief in Jesus' kindness and mercy, in his acceptance of *all* mortals into heaven—sinful or not.

Although Anne later set out to fight rigorous Calvinistic dogma, believing consciously in the Wesleyan view (humanity's salvation through Jesus Christ), conflict and doubt are, nevertheless, present in her unconscious. Such noxious strife surfaces at crucial periods in her life, when psychologically she is most vulnerable. Her profound disquietude is reminiscent of some of the metaphysical poems of John Donne (1572–1631): "Batter My Heart," "Death Be Not Proud,""Hymne to God the Father." His yearning for union with god and his obsession with death and sin frequently filled him as well with doubts relative to salvation.

Although she broods and is burdened with "sin and woe," moroseness is lifted in the poem, "Confidence." Anne's energies are rekindled through the power of reason: "Opposed by many a mighty foe: / But I will not despair"; and in "When sink my heart in hopeless gloom," Anne now is confident that serenity and bliss await her after her years of suffering—in another world.

Anne's fixated need of God's love is ever present, most particularly during moments of disquietude, when doubt in His existence fosters dread and spiritual despondency. "In Memory of a Happy day in February" is a meditation on God's capacity for mercy, as her world suddenly takes on, in mitigated form, the glow of beauty and joy. God's countenance no longer fills her with terror; she is certain of resurrection.

No matter the calming feelings of serenity that enclothe Anne, anguish always returns along with doubt, gnawing and tempestuous in their torturing effect: "O God! if this indeed be all." When the agony of existence seems to overwhelm her, the sterility of her world and its utter loneliness becomes all-encompassing. Then Anne seemingly yearns for death.

Although finding release in depicting nature in such forces as flowers, here too she is stark in her economy of words; frugal in her decanting of emotions. Her powerful bouts with anguish seem to diminish in power as she gazes at the unending beauty and excitement of God's creation. The loving pantheism implicit in "The Bluebell," a contemplative poem, restores hope in Anne's heart. Merging with the living and visible forms burgeoning all around her, be it in the wild dramatic landscape of the moors, or the subdued, controlled, and delicate growth of flowers in a Yorkshire garden, she seems ready to breathe in these health-provoking forces.

Was poetry a compensatory device for Anne? Was it a way of dealing with her pain and her struggle for serenity? Was it a consolation for her many days and nights given over to loneliness? Certainly, the very nature of the poetic process not only afforded her periods of intense joy, but held out to her ways and means of externalizing, synthesizing, and eternalizing her most obsessive thoughts and most personal grievances in the form of impersonal lamentations and hymns.

THE NOVELS

Agnes Grey: "The Power and the Will to Be Useful"

George Moore wrote that *Agnes Grey* (1847) was "the most perfect prose narrative in English literature.... [It] is a narrative simple and beautiful as a muslin dress."[5] Although somewhat exaggerated, Moore's statement nevertheless captured certain of Anne's literary qualities. *Agnes Gray*, which relates the painful story of a governess's difficulties with her self-centered class-conscious employers and their undisciplined and willful children, is structured to perfection. Meticulously plotted, its division into two main sequences—covering the protagonist's two posts as governess in two environments, and two religious experiences—is dramatically simple and direct. Although seemingly restrained in narration and in dialogue sequences, this partially autobiographical novel seethes with fervor and passion. Written in full consciousness of her theme, Anne is mistress of her material, as she is of herself. When pain and humiliation surge, the author sees fit to discuss these feelings; the same is true of bouts of incipient enthusiasm and idealism. A less-composed and -disciplined writer might not have written so clearly and concisely. The authors of so many novels of the day too often waxed in "tearful" and sentimental interludes, as they allowed their protagonists to be overwhelmed by feelings of alienation and humiliation.

That *Agnes Grey*, as Moore noted, is a novel "simple and beautiful as a muslin dress," is rigorously perceptive: "simple" in its depiction of personalities, each delineated with the deftness and expertise of a craftsman; "beautiful" in Anne's interdisciplinary use of nature as a backdrop reflecting the protagonist's moods. Darkness, bleakness, storm clouds, or windswept seas convey feelings of sorrow and solitude; ordered and planned gardens, walks, groves, and parks express uniformity and systematization and thus safety; cruelty toward people or animals mirror rage and anger, as well as fear of sin and damnation. Events are planned to create suspense and reach a climax, expanding the depth and breadth of the *learning* experience that was, for Anne, the goal of her writing.

Moore's metaphor of the "dress" is equally insightful. Characters, nature, and incidents are all used to clothe or cover what the modest and puritanical Anne seeks to mask: her private *feeling* realm. Love and hatred, serenity and anger, superiority and inferiority, kindness and meanness, generosity and egotism, dependency and independence are projected onto her characters with deftness and dexterity. By concretizing these feelings, Anne may unconsciously be facing both sides of her personality, thus beginning to divest herself of those "ungodly" traits. She might find it easier to manipulate traits, such as arrogance and self-centeredness in her characters by categorizing good and evil rather simplistically under two polarities. Thus if Evil is implicit in a protagonist, it can be condemned and rejected. Observed from a psychological point of view, *Agnes Gray* depicts a medley of warring polarities, reflecting its author's highly complex psyche.

Written in the first person, *Agnes Grey* tells the story of the naive, idealistic, and inexperienced nineteen-year-old daughter of a poor parson who, to help her family financially, takes a post as governess. Her first employers, the Bloomfields, are tradespeople, the parents of three undisciplined, cruel, willful and egotistical children. Humiliated after failing to teach them properly and to redress their callous ways, Agnes is summarily dismissed. Determined to prove herself, she takes another job as governess to the four Murray children of Horton Lodge. Although each in his or her own way is a conceited and spoiled tormentor and prevaricator, the governess remains with the family for nearly four years, to discover that Mrs. Murray is flighty and a social climber, prone to playing favorites among her children, and encouraging her daughters to seek wealth and title rather than love from a future husband. Agnes's ire and disdain for Mr. Hatfield, the vicar of the parish, are unsparing. His hypocritical and materialistic motivations are set against the humble, altruistic, and noble comportment of the curate, Edward Weston. After the conventional peripeteias and time lapses, Agnes marries Weston and they and their children live happily ever after.

The Feminist: "I Must Stand Alone"

Subdued, but not passive; reserved, but not weak; patient, but not without fire—Anne had been deeply preoccupied not only with moral problems, but social ones as well. Regarding the plight and working conditions of the unmarried girl and women who are obliged to go out into the world and earn a living, Agnes constantly battles to eradicate dishonesty and misbehavior and to raise the standards, salaries, and treatment of female employees.

The intent of her narrative—to instruct—is clear from the opening sentence of *Agnes Grey:* "All true histories contain instruction; though, in some, the treasure may be hard to find, and when found, so trivial in quantity that the dry, shrivelled kernel scarcely compensates for the trouble of cracking the nut."[6]

Experience, Anne realizes, is the best of teachers: it broadens and deepens the individual and brings insights into the outer world and oneself: "How little know we what we are / How less what we may be."[7]

Like some other didactic feminist novels of the century, such as Maria Edgeworth's *The Parent's Assistant* (1796–1800), Harriet Martineau's *Deerbrook* (1839), Mary Taylor's *Miss Miles; or, A Tale of Yorkshire Life Sixty Years Ago* (1890), and Elizabeth Missing Sewell's *Amy Herbert* (1844), Anne also preached woman's education as the first step toward her economic independence and self-respect. For Anne, perhaps even more so than for the other feminists of her day, instruction became a vocation—a mission in the religious sense of the word—and not merely an avocation.

Anne was determined—as is a missionary—to reform the plight of the governess who was not only underpaid for her services, but looked down upon and badly treated by her employers and, as a result, by their children and the other servants in the household. Searching for ways to help the growing number of unmarried women find adequate, it not always fulfilling situations, she used the novel as her way of altering society's negative view of the working woman in general. Because of the fact that there was a decreasing number of men in the 1840s, more women remained celibate and thus dependent upon family or charity. The literature of the day was filled with the problems of the spinster, of the girl without a dowry who had little or no hope of finding a suitable husband, of the uneducated girl who could look forward to no more than being a housemaid, a cook, laundress,

milliner, seamstress, or factory worker. The well-educated girl
might become a tutor, teacher, or secretary, and of course, girls
could emigrate to New Zealand, Australia, the United States, or
elsewhere, as many of them did. Charlotte Brontë's friend, Mary
Taylor, considering the lot of the unmarried woman in England to
be outrageous, emigrated to New Zealand.

As more women sought employment, competition grew increasingly acute and good jobs were extremely difficult to obtain. Salaries were concomitantly lowered to such a point as to be hardly
sufficient to house, feed, and clothe an unmarried woman. The
Bloomfields, Agnes Grey's first employer, although wealthy, paid
her only twenty-five pounds a year; the Murrays, fifty pounds,
out of which Agnes paid for her clothes, laundry, postage, statio-
nery, and journeys home, which amounted to twenty-seven
pounds a year.

Although novels focusing on the plight of the governess became
popular in Victorian England, *Agnes Grey*, unlike the Countess
Marguerite Blessington's highly romantic narrative, *The Governess* (1839), is written unsentimentally, from the head. Readers learn
of the trials and tribulations of the governess, and of her social
status, in a relatively objective and factual manner; they will be
invited to peer into the protagonist's heart, but via a strategy of
events, relationships, and situations as analyzed by Agnes. Despite
humiliations and wrongs meted out to her—resulting in her withdrawal into the intimacy of her room to weep—affects are released consciously and in private, never irrationally or in public.
What was the lesson a governess had to learn? "To stand alone,"
that is, to be independent, despite the coldness, the calumnies,
and the degradation employers might foist upon her.

Life's Educational Process: "Seasoned in Adversity"

A chill in the air, cold, and icy surroundings pervade the atmosphere from the moment the protagonist leaves her warm and loving home to the time she arrives at her first post as governess at
the Bloomfield estate, where she is welcomed by a grave, forbidding, scornful Mrs. Bloomfield, whose "frigid formality" sets the
tenor for Agnes's painful adventure. Although terrified at first,
Agnes is determined to fulfill her mission as governess/educator.
Because her Christian evangelical upbringing had taught her to
dedicate her life to doing good works, discipline, self-control, and
a highly developed sense of morality are her governing principles.

When a sense of sin and imminent judgment are implicit in the events narrated in *Agnes Grey*, terror and anguish prevail in the protagonist's daily existence, encouraging her to become more rigid in her manner and increasingly doctrinaire in her point of view. When more positive Wesleyan values take over, and salvation through faith in Jesus Christ holds sway, Agnes is hopeful for the future and focuses on more positive ways of character building, though perhaps nearly equally rigorous in method. No less an authority than John Wesley, the founder of Methodism, stated in reference to children's education: "Break their wills betimes, begin this work before they can run alone, before they can speak plain, perhaps before they can speak at all. Whatever pains it costs, break the will, if you would not damn the child."[8]

Most important for Agnes, as for Anne, was moral comportment and the enactment of good deeds coming from the heart. What the protagonist had not counted upon were the changes taking place in England's educational theories and systems, possibly inspired by Jean-Jacques Rousseau's *Émile* (1762). Mrs. Bloomfield, an adherent of the new approach, had misinterpreted the theories of Rousseau, who had advocated learning by experience and observation, physical exercise, the mastery of useful trades, the development of judgment, and hard work—all of which were to be carried out by a warm and loving preceptor and in a pleasant and joyful atmosphere. The uninformed Mrs. Robinson, understanding only that she must spare the rod, forbad Agnes to reprimand, punish, or curtail her children's freedom in any way, unheedful of Rousseau's dictum that a warm, loving, and positive environment must be created. Tom, aged seven, Mary Ann, six, and Fanny, four, were encouraged by their mother to express their feelings and needs freely and indulge their every whim. In no way was Agnes allowed to thwart their desires. Problems became overt from the very outset. Denied all authority, forbidden to punish the children or even discuss their faults with anyone but Mrs. Bloomfield, Agnes was powerless to deal with these unruly young people under her supervision.

Tom, the problem child, was bright but intellectually lazy. Because he was the only boy and the strongest of the four, each time the spirit of rebellion overtook him, he encouraged the others to follow suit. Having decided to refuse to study, for example, he convinced his sisters they should close their books and put down their work. The result? All were backward in their reading and writing skills. Agnes, persevering and determined, pitted against her enemy, the children, forswore giving up: "by dint of great labour and patience . . . [she] managed to get something done in the course of the morning." Nevertheless, with each passing day Agnes found herself pitted against the children, thus making instruction increasingly arduous. She was clever enough, however, to realize that a teacher, unless prepared to carry out her threats and promises, must never resort to such strategies to enforce her will. The only effective means she had of taming these "wild" children was to play on their fear of their father. The mere mention of his name called them to obedience.

Despite Agnes's educational setbacks and the many insults and humiliations she suffered at the hands of her employers, her faith in her ability to overcome obstacles increased. By making the children aware of their sins, gently and with "perfect kindness," she was convinced that, in the end, she would surmount their spirit of opposition. Her weapons, in addition to "Divine Assistance," would be "Patience, Firmness, and Perseverance." Agnes's glorious method was not, however, always effective; Tom, in particular, frequently refused simply to listen. When ordered to do something, he would just stand before Agnes, "twisting his body and face into the most grotesque and singular contortions." The other children, understandably, would burst out laughing. Their "yells and doleful outcries" were certainly intended to provoke Agnes. She however resisted the temptation: "I might inwardly tremble with impatience and irritation, I manfully strove to suppress all visible signs of molestation, and affected to sit, with calm indifference." There were moments, however, when Agnes, at wits' end, realized that "In vain I argued, coaxed, entreated, threatened, scolded," trying to dominate the "absurd perversity" of the children. Then Agnes finally lost control of herself—and this was a rarity—she sometimes shook Mary Ann violently by the shoulders, or pulled her long hair, or put her in the corner. Reacting to such punishments, and attempting to seek revenge upon her tormentor, the vindictive Mary Ann, knowing that her governess hated shrieks, would let out "loud, shrill, piercing screams that went through [Agnes's] head like a knife." In vain did Agnes wait for any "symptoms of contrition," any feelings of regret.

Mr. Bloomfield's comportment toward Agnes was as rude and as crude as was that of his offspring. Unlike the gracious and courteous Victorian families depicted so frequently in fiction, Mr. & Mrs. Bloomfield were mean, defiant, self-centered, and unfeeling toward others, and even toward each other. They were oblivious to the concerns of their employees, especially the female ones. Indeed, Mrs. Robinson's brother, a "scorner of the female sex," adopted a "supercilious insolence of tone and manner" that offended Agnes on several occasions. It was he, she felt, who encouraged the children's "evil propensities." On one occasion, when Agnes found Tom torturing little birds, she tried to make him stop the mutilation, but he was deaf to her wishes. Out of desperation, and seeking to end their suffering instantaneously, she killed the birds quickly with a stone. Tom's cruelty toward animals, she reasoned, was symptomatic of his outlook on life.

Agnes's moral rectitude and her conviction that her understanding of right and wrong was the correct one, gave her the strength to commit a mercy killing, thus ending injury of a sentient creature. No animal, including a bird, she told the children, was "created for our convenience." Nor does anyone have the right to torment anything or anyone for his amusement. Quoting from Matthew, she said: "Blessed are the merciful, for they shall obtain mercy" (5:7). When informed of the incident, rather than chastise her son for his ferocity, Mrs. Bloomfield blamed Agnes for her reprehensible act. Indeed, her "aspect and demeanor were doubly dark and chill" as she informed the governess that after midsummer, Agnes's services would no longer be required.

Not only were the Bloomfields completely oblivious to the meaning of shame, Agnes noted, but they were devoid of any and all kindness, affection, or feeling. Coldness alone permeated their manner, congelation their feeling principle. Before her departure, Agnes accorded herself only one luxury: at night, in weakness, she yielded to "an unrestricted burst of weeping."

Loneliness and alienation had marked Agnes's first experience away from home. She might have more accurately predicted her fate as she left her warm and loving home on that raw and dreary day for the Bloomfields'. Riding in the gig, ascending and descending hills and vales, she looked back frequently to her village and its spires. She considered the "slanting beam of sunshine" to be a propitious omen. Yet it was "a sickly ray" and "the village and surrounding hills were all in sombre shade." Nature's dark and solemn aspects, she might have realized, were in the ascendance. Then, suddenly, when she could no longer see her home and its surrounding moors, a stinging sensation struck her. Cut off from family and friends, and all of her loved ones, Agnes realized she would be forced to face *reality* for the first time;

henceforth, her life would be shorn of that wonderful childhood world of fantasy and fiction.

The trip to the Bloomfield estate had been a leap into ice, distance, impersonality, and cruelty. Nevertheless, she had mettle. Rather than being devastated by the loss of her post, the months spent at the Bloomfields' that had been so emotionally draining, particularly since she had no sister with whom she could confide, she found another source of comfort. Agnes learned to indwell, to rely on her own reserves for strength and solace. She discovered a storehouse of treasures within her very being, concluding that she had been "seasoned by adversity." With increased courage she forged ahead, noting in silence that "Unshaken firmness, devoted diligence, unwearied perseverance, unceasing care were the very qualifications on which I had secretly prided myself."

No longer was she to be identified with weakness and passivity. On the contrary, she felt invigorated by her ordeal. Her employment at the Bloomfields' had forced her to mature, she concluded. It had taught her to take an independent stand and to relate to others more strongly and effectively than ever before. Agnes was still to suffer bouts of anxiety and agitation, but she had dealt and would increasingly learn to deal with difficult situations in a more effective manner. Her continuous readings of the Bible had perhaps prepared her to consider humanity's cruelties as tests sent by God to strengthen her faith: "despise not the chastening of the Lord; neither be weary of his corrections: For whom the Lord loveth he correcteth; even as a father the son in whom he delighteth" (Prov. 3:11–12).

Certainly, Agnes's dedication and faith had been tested at the Bloomfields'; it would again be tried at the Murrays'. Wiser this time, and because she had listened to her mother's sage advice— he who does not esteem himself is not esteemed by others—she had high hopes for the future. Agnes understood the importance of developing her self-confidence and thus becoming aware of her self-worth. Nor, she realized, were her qualifications negligible: she was capable of teaching music, singing, drawing, French, Latin, and German.

Self-worth: "A Wide, White Wilderness"

Agnes's second venture into the outside world may again be interpreted through nature. Was it an ominous sign that, on the day of her departure, a "strong north wind" blew and the "continual storm of snow drifting on the ground and whirling through the air" was "wild" and "tempestuous"? Darkness and congelation again prevailed, as it had on the day of her departure for the Bloomfields'. Another element, however, imposed itself in her second foray into the world away from home: the whiteness of the landscape introduced a note of purity and beauty into the scheme of things.

Less naïve now, Agnes had learned to be both optimistic and pessimistic, neither one to the exclusion of the other. She was, therefore, resigned in part to the icy reception, the materialism, and the corruption she was certain would greet her at the Murrays'. Still, her evangelical side would urge her to reform people's comportment in the hope of inculcating into them a sense of morality and integrity. Despite feelings of utter "desolation" that forever invaded her when thrust into a new environment, she sought to rectify what otherwise could have led to a crucial imbalance within her. Her strong willpower enabled her to reestablish some semblance of harmony within her psyche and keep her feelings and actions in check. Only on retiring to her bedroom did she allow her repressed emotions full sway. On cold days, warmed by a small "smouldering fire" in the hearth, she would allow herself the pleasure of a good cry, after which she said her prayers and went to bed.

The Murrays differed significantly from the Bloomfields. A "blustering, roistering, country squire," Mr. Murray, a bon vivant, devoted his time to fox hunting and farming. Unlike the cold and distant Mrs. Bloomfield, the forty-year-old Mrs. Murray "was a handsome, dashing lady" who enjoyed parties and fashion. Agnes's teaching obligations would also be dissimilar. Although her teaching hours were increased, she was disappointed because *real learning* was not the parents' objective. She was directed to cram as much Latin grammar, arithmetic, and other disciplines as possible into the heads of the two boys, while the girls were to learn the social graces and sufficient rudiments of the arts to enhance their attractiveness to young men of high society.

Difficulties with regard to Agnes's teaching methods began almost at the outset. The Murray boys were as headstrong, violent, and unprincipled as those of her former employer. Their mischievous natures were also indulged by their mother as were their "malicious wantonness" and frequent falsehoods. That music, singing, dancing, French, and German were to be taught the three girls with the *sole* purpose of enhancing their charm, refinement,

polish, and social graces ran counter to Agnes's straitlaced views.
The cultivation of the mind was designed to increase one's knowledge, and was not to be viewed only as an ornament to be added
to one's accomplishments, which, Agnes believed, was hypocritical—a sham. Increasing her discomfiture was the fact that Mrs.
Murray had forbidden her—as had the Bloomfields—from exer-
cising her authority. "Persuasion and gentle remonstrance" alone
were acceptable.

Agnes still considered herself "an alien among strangers," but
her increased maturity had made her more aware of the differences that prevailed between her, as employee, and her employers
and their children. To her surprise, her greater self-esteem had
served to make her even more vulnerable to insults, slights, denigrating mannerisms and remarks. Unwilling or unable to believe
the evidence, she could not accept the fact that she had been hired
for the sole purpose of performing a function. Her hurt chafed
from the very start, from the moment she noted that Mrs. Murray, so intent upon seeing to the happiness of her children, "never
once mentioned" any thought of Agnes's needs or welfare.

The differences between Agnes's values and those of the Murrays also served to widen the line of demarcation between them.
She felt "abused" and put-upon because she was never consulted
in matters of judgment, yet her sense of commitment and her faith
in her ability to succeed instilled in her a powerful sense of obligation that drove her on. She was determined to inculcate higher
standards into her young wards, to teach them to moderate their
desires, to temper and bridle their instincts, and above all, to sacrifice their personal pleasures for the good of the others.

Only with Rosalie Murray, the beautiful, tall, and slender
sixteen-year-old daughter, did Agnes build a semblance of a relationship. At first "cold and haughty" to the "poor curate's daughter," Rosalie grew to "respect" her, and, in time, even become
attached to her. Agnes at first found Rosalie's conceited and friv-
olous behavior most shocking. Anathema to her was the young
lady's need to attract young men in order to conquer their hearts
only to reject them. The pleasure she derived from this kind of
"game" was heartless, Agnes told her; one must never trifle with
the feelings of others. That Rosalie's marriage to a titled and
wealthy young man failed after but one year—she was no longer
able to abide her husband and he became utterly indifferent to
her—was, to Agnes's mind, an example of Divine intervention.

The Ministry

Agnes's indignation was aimed not only at her employers and their progeny, but at those involved in the ministry. Mr. Hatfield, the vicar, who observed *all* the rules and regulations outwardly, represented everything that was detestable in the established church. His sermons and hellfire orations were designed to inspire fear and not love in his congregation. He saw "Deity as a terrible task-master, rather than a benevolent father" and was unable to abide dissent. Total obedience to *his* interpretation of church law had to be observed to the letter. Personal thought was not permitted. Repugnant to Agnes were his exhibitionism, his hypocrisy, his attempts to ingratiate himself with the wealthy and influential parishioners, and his contempt for the poor.[9] In one of Anne's gnomic depictions, she writes as follows of Mr. Hatfield:

[He] would come sailing up the aisle, or rather sweeping along like a whirlwind, with his rich silk gown flying behind . . . mount the pulpit like a conqueror ascending his triumphal car; then sinking on the velvet cushion in an attitude of studied grace, remain in silent prostration for a certain time; then, mutter over a Collect, and gabble through the Lord's Prayer, rise, draw off one bright lavender glove to give the congregation the benefit of his sparkling rings, lightly pass his fingers through his well-curled hair, flourish a cambric handkerchief . . .

In sharp contrast to the vicar was the curate, Mr. Weston, who visited the cottages of the poor and the sick, ministering to their needs and comforting them. His readings of the Bible filled his flock with feelings of warmth and belonging: "He that loveth not, knoweth not God." He neither condemned his parishioners nor aroused fear in them as was Mr. Hatfield's manner. The curate's reasoning was that "He that is born of God cannot commit sin." Mr. Weston's approach to the suffering and those in want was not limited to words alone, but included deeds as well. He sent his parishioners food and coal when these were in short supply, paying for such gifts out of his own meager salary.

The more Agnes saw of Mr. Weston and learned firsthand of his kindnesses, the deeper ran her feelings for him. Unlike Mr. Hatfield or the Murrays, Mr. Weston showed great concern for her well-being, his delicacy and tenderness toward her manifesting themselves in an exquisite little scene. One day, as Agnes was returning to the Murrays' she saw a clump of primroses that reminded her of those that grew at home; the glow of warmth and love she associated with her family was so strongly felt that she had a sudden urge to pick them. Try as she might, she failed to reach them. About to despair, she heard Mr. Weston's voice behind her. Startled at first by his unexpected presence, she graciously accepted his offer to pick them for her. Unaccustomed to such attention, she deemed his gesture to be an added jewel to adorn his already exemplary character.

After leaving the Murrays' employ, Agnes did not see Mr. Weston again. She busied herself by founding her own school not far from her home. One day, as if destiny had seen fit to instill joy into her life, she chanced upon the curate. After renewing their friendship, Agnes introduced the curate to her mother and family. In due course he proposed marriage and she accepted. They had three children and lived in bliss thereafter.

Although a novel with a message, its heroine being the purveyor of truth, morality, and reform, *Agnes Grey* is far from being cut and dried. Nor is it maudlin or self-indulgent. Its crisp sentences are to the point, and endowed with rhythmic and imagistic variety. The strategies aimed at eliciting pity from the reader and creating suspense are neither cumbersome nor artificial. On the contrary, the seemingly effortless and harmonious change from narration to description, to commentary, to confession, lends subdued and unaffected drams to the sequences. Events and characters encourage the reader to probe and evaluate the protagonist's self-conscious, analytical, but paradoxically passionate, personality. Commitment and intransigence, rectitude and rigidity, are weapons that help Agnes cope with her feelings of alienation, solitude, and profound humiliation. Pain, conveyed internally, never overtly, is presented as a fact of life to test the power of her evangelical missionary qualities. Agnes's religious convictions gave her the strength to bear the ignominies, insults, and wayward ways of those with whom she had come into contact.

Rather than underscoring their aesthetic reactions to *Agnes Grey*, mid-Victorian critics focused on the moral issues at stake. The reviewer for the *New Monthly Magazine* preferred *Agnes Grey* to the novels of both Emily and Charlotte because "its language is less ambitious and less repulsive, it fills the mind with a lasting picture of love and happiness succeeding to scorn and affliction, and teaches us to put every trust in a supreme wisdom and goodness." Along a similar vein ran the comments of the reviewer for the *Atlas: Agnes Grey* "is a tale of everyday life, and though not wholly free from exaggeration (there are some detestable young ladies in it), does not offend by any startling improbabilities. It is more level and more sunny. Perhaps we shall best describe it as a somewhat coarse imitation of one of Miss Austin's [sic] charming stories.[10]"

The Tenant of Wildfell Hall: "Unpalatable Truth"

George Moore's high praise for *The Tenant of Wildfell Hall* (1848) was limited to the first hundred and fifty pages: the "weaving of the narrative reveals a born story-teller"; its "breakdown was not for lack of genius but of experience."[11] While Anne's first novel dealt with the mission of teaching and rectification of abuse toward the governesses as employee, *The Tenant*, also didactic but far from ponderous in nature, focuses on evils such as alcoholism, profligacy, and self-indulgence. Unlike *Agnes Grey*, which is a simple and straightforward novel and the outgrowth of a personal experience, *The Tenant*, far more complex in its panoply of personalities and plot lines, seems somewhat contrived. The artifice implicit in the passionate love scenes creates a stilted atmosphere that simply does not ring true. On the other hand, the poignancy of the protagonist's agony as she witnesses her husband's increasing addiction to alcohol and gambling is deeply felt, and undoubtedly was modeled on Anne's observation of Branwell's alcoholism and use of opiates as well as his disastrous love affair with Mrs. Robinson.

Anne's depictions of love scenes are surprising and unexpected: couples touch each other, kiss, and anticipate further sensual delights. By today's standards, such evocations go unobserved. In Anne's day, however, imagistic detailing of this kind of event was virtually taboo. Could other, perhaps unconscious motivations, have played a role in Anne's inclusion of such "daring" scenes? She shrank before nothing: "I will speak it," she stated categorically in the second preface to *The Tenant*. The very strength and courage already noted in *Agnes Grey* may have prodded her to go still further in stating the truth as she saw it in some marital relationships. Anne had learned a great deal after stepping out of her circumscribed world of the parsonage. Her two posts as governess, although unpleasant for the most part, were nutritive in that they permitted confrontation with the *real* world, thus fostering growth. Exposed to foreign and frequently antipathetic moral and ideological ways, she learned that infidelity, rancor, jealousy, materialism, and cruelty between husband and wife were not only the stuff of fiction, but were rampant in the existential world. Although Anne was repulsed by such ignominious comportment, to write about it so extensively must have presented some kind of unconscious attraction to her—like forbidden fruit.

From Branwell's behavior, as well as that of her employers and their friends, Anne learned secondhand the meaning of *desire* and *sexual* attraction. To dwell on sinful sensual delights for the purpose of pointing up the evils involved allowed her to live the experience vicariously, thereby exposing herself to those latent but very real sensations within her own being. Sight must not be lost of the fact that Anne had ardently wanted to marry and have children. That she accomplished neither and probably knew in her heart that she would not, might have triggered in her an unconscious morbid fascination with pleasurable/forbidden eroticism. While exploring the multiple relationships in her novel, *The Tenant,* explaining the continuously altering love/hate sequences, she *lived them,* perhaps even quivering with anticipation. Noteworthy are the shifting rhythmic qualities of her sentences: lilting and choppy during tempestuous moments; harmonious and sustained during periods of serenity.

The atmosphere Anne creates in *The Tenant* is melded with her ideology. No sooner does the pleasure principle surface—considered evil according to her conscious outlook—than it is summarily repressed. When Good, Light, Kindness, and Perfection prevail, and Heaven may be accorded the sinner at Judgment, torment diminishes and the possibility of Hell's fires are dispelled. Dangers, nevertheless, are in store. To seek perfection, as does Anne's heroine, is not only to divide a human psyche, but also to call its opposite, sin, into activity. To vie for absolute perfection and purity is to create an *inhuman* or godlike figure, thus denigrating and finally destroying a person's earthly side by relegating it to animal status where instinct alone prevails.

Psychological imbalance comes into play with an overemphasis of spirituality and a concomitant rejection of instinctuality. It divests one of the enriching *soil* of life. Nothing grows in *absolute* purity/sterility. The murky and sordid side of life, which Anne experienced through her brother and some of the personalities she had met when working as governess, enabled her better to understand and examine the meaning of life's "evil earthly" content.

Anne lived others' passions vicariously, thus indulging in what psychoanalysts term, "substitute formation," indicating a need in her to discharge repressed impulses indirectly—that is, via another person or in her writing. Let me note that the love motifs in *Agnes Grey* were divested of all sensuality and reality, confirming the fact that Anne would never admit to what she had denied or repressed. That she was drawn to the whole sexual side of life in *The Tenant,* which she considered fundamentally abhorrent, gives her the opportunity of negating such "base" procedures. Viewed psychologically, such rejection of sexuality may be looked upon as a kind of primitive defense mechanism designed to preserve her from contamination.

Since denial suggests an unconscious intent to ignore information presented to the perceptory system and memory apparatus, "substitute formation" as a defense mechanism functions at its best in undeveloped psyches. The energy emerging from the instinctual world is thus warded off by displacement onto another person and/or connection to other experiences. Surfacing, it catalyzes new associations, thus serving to increase the intensity of the affect while also transforming its quality in the process. There are many scenes in *The Tenant,* for example, in which the protagonist, while denying all "sinful" sensual proclivities, nevertheless delights in her fiancé's, and later in her husband's glances, smiles, and blushing ardour, unconsciously longing to possess the power of attraction that other women have.

The Tenant is two-thirds epistolary and one-third confessional. Part 1 consists of letters from Gilbert Markham, a twenty-four-year-old gentlemen farmer who lives on his estate, probably in Yorkshire, to his talkative mother, sullen brother, and attractive sister. In a series of flashbacks, he details the events of his life from autumn 1827 to the following summer, telling of the arrival of a new tenant—the mysterious widow, Helen Huntingdon, and her young son, Arthur—at Wildfell Hall, a once-elegant mansion that has now fallen to ruin. Helen's meeting with the narrator sends his heart aflutter. For some unknown reason, she keeps him at a distance. Gossipmongers are fast at work calumniating the young widow, spreading ugly rumors about her morals. Markham refuses to listen. Although attracted to him, Helen not only represses her feelings, but rejects his marriage proposal. When, one evening, Markham sees her walking arm in arm on her estate with his friend, Lawrence, he is outraged and believes the gossip he has heard. After confronting her, she attempts to exculpate herself by asking him to read her diary that relates events in her life from 1821–27. In part 2, we learn from Helen's diary that her mother had died when she was an infant, that her father drank, and that she had been raised by her uncle, a reformed roué, and her very religious aunt. Against her aunt's advice, she married the highly seductive Arthur Huntingdon. Upon discovering, only three months after her wedding, that Arthur was a rake, gambler, drunkard, and adulterer, she took it into her head to reform him. Although aware of his comportment during his lengthy trips to London, and his behavior toward some of their female guests, namely, Annabella, the wife of a friend of theirs, she bore her cross in silence. Only when her husband hired a so-called governess, in reality his mistress, to care for their son, did Helen decide to flee with her son and live at Wildfell Hall. A gifted artist, she thought she would be able to earn enough money to support herself and her son by selling her paintings. Discovering her plan, her husband burned her canvases, took her jewels and all her money. Helen then called upon her brother, Lawrence, whom Markham had thought to be her lover, to help her escape. Part 3, a continuation of Markham's missives to a friend, also includes some of Helen's to him: thus do we read a series of letters within letters. When Helen, now living at Wildfell Hall, learns that her husband's terminal illness results from his excesses, she returns to his bedside and cares for him during his last hours.

"I Will Speak It"

Helen, a righteous and God-fearing Christian, is determined to fight for good over evil, for God versus Satan. Her purpose is to convert others to her way of thinking, thus fostering light and obliterating darkness. Although convinced of the reality of evil and of sin, Helen is equally certain of pardon and salvation. Because she believes that everything on earth has a divine purpose, Hell's fires are viewed as purgative, and therefore have a positive function.

While on the surface her mode of thinking seems positive, its destructive side is also evident. She becomes increasingly imprisoned in her dogmatic, constricting, and intransigent ideology, dominated as she is her idée fixe: to save her husband's soul. Her overt sanctity is guaranteed to take the life out of any marriage, as indeed it does to hers.[12]

The first months after Helen becomes Mrs. Huntingdon, the couple lives at Grassdale Manor, the husband's gorgeous country estate. She busies herself with her artwork, reading, letter writing, and household duties, while he goes out riding or hunting. No problems arise on sunny days; only when rain makes it impossible for him to go out of doors does he feel boredom, having no occupation, hobbies, or interests. So foreign is his personality to Helen's that, rather than try to understand his needs, she preaches and nags at him: he *must* strengthen himself against temptation, he *must* think more deeply and aim higher. Such admonitions not only make him feel uneasy and insecure, but in time annoy him. Husband and wife quarrel readily. To drive away his feelings of inadequacy and boredom, he begins drinking wine. Oblivious to these signals and despite the fact that she had known about his heavy drinking and womanizing prior to their marriage, she pursues her sanctimonious ways. He, given to evil, must follow her lead and become all pure, all light, all integrity.

At the outset of their marriage, Huntingdon had made efforts to give up his wild ways and for several months had succeeded; Helen, however, had not altered her program of conversion. Although she was beautiful and charming, her moral rigidity, ultra-religiosity, and perhaps even frigidity, were intractable. Her quest for purity must have palled on him, for on several occasions he made it clear to her that he was *not* religious and did not even know the implications of such a term. However, he liked women to be churchgoers; it added to their charm, he told her, provided they did not carry it to the extreme. Disregarding both the meaning implicit in his statement as well as his sexual attraction toward her, she again emphasizes *soul food* rather than *physical contact*. Unruffled and unaware of the one-sided nature of her relationship with him, Helen discourses on and on. When Huntingdon tells her not "to be so hard" on him and not to "pinch" his arm so because she is squeezing her "fingers into the bone," the metaphor he uses to underscore his point of view is not only misunderstood, but not even heard, so locked is she in her own moral prerogatives. Her didacticism is such that when he confesses his fear that she might not love him, she responds as usual from her head rather than from her heart.

Predictably, Helen's intransigence and arrogance cannot but help force him back to his old "sin-ridden" comportment. As she is the paragon of virtue, the only one to know the *right* way, the chasm between husband and wife grows ever wider. Had she displayed a measure of humility, had she attempted to put herself in his place rather than withdraw into her stonelike cell, she might have been able to discover a storehouse of riches within his personality. Unable to do so, she pursues her credo: any deviation from her *straight and narrow path* spells *evil*. She, like so many one-sided individuals regardless of their credo, is convinced that she is privy to God's truths.[13]

When Helen first accompanies her husband to London and finds herself unable to bear his life-style, she returns to Grassdale Manor alone while he, intent upon remaining in the big city, enjoys his flings. When he does come back to Grassdale, a month or two later, he finds himself constrained to listen to her reprimands and homiletics. The tighter she ties the noose, the more urgent he feels the need for release. His departures for London become more and more frequent and last for longer periods of time. To encourage her husband not to leave home, Helen invites his friends to the manor. Some of the guests Huntingdon entertains, however, are of his own ilk—fast livers, who enjoy alcohol and womanizing. Only after the birth of their son, Arthur, does their situation grow untenable. Her aunt had been right, Helen admits to herself, when she had tried to dissuade her from marrying such a sinner. She cannot, however, turn back the clock: "Whatever *I ought* to have done, my duty, now, is plainly to love him and to cleave to him; and this just tallies with my inclination."

The "Degrading Vice" of Alcoholism

Although Helen is aware of her husband's growing intemperance and violence when under the effects of liquor, she still seeks to save him from this "degrading vice." After each of his bouts, at home or in London, she slowly concludes that her system is failing and that he is growing increasingly irritable and irascible in her company. Along with psychological changes, she notes a physical alteration in him: the once-handsome, vigorous, and vivacious man had become flushed, feverish, listless, and wan.

"Arthur, you *must* repent," Helen says. Rather than taking her advice, he pursues his "depraved" actions. When drink, drugs, and womanizing have gotten out of hand, she asks permission to leave with their child and what remains of her fortune. He, of course, answers in the negative, declaring that his pride would be hurt and, moreover, he would be the talk of the land. Only now does Helen understand the role she plays in his life: "I am your child's mother, and *your* housekeeper—nothing more." No love exists between them any longer. In fact, she bursts out, "It is not enough to say that I no longer love my husband—I hate him!" She hates him because of his "sinful" ways that she has unwittingly encouraged in part.

The day Helen decides to leave her husband's estate with her son, her jewelry, and her paintings, a member of the household, probably the governess (Hungtingdon's mistress), plays informer. Bursting in on Helen, her husband grabs the key to her private secretary, takes her jewels, money, and burns her canvases, making her more determined than ever to leave. She refuses to allow her son to be *contaminated* by the influence of her husband or his friends. With her brother's help, she and her son slip out to safety at night.

When, sometime later, she learns that he is dying from an internal inflammation brought on by overindulgence, her anger is transformed into compassion and grief. She and Arthur rush to his bedside where they remain night and day still providing him with the same homiletics, begging him to repent.

"I *can't* repent; I only fear."
"Think of the goodness of God, and you cannot but be grieved to have offended Him."
"What is God—I cannot see him or hear Him?—God is only an idea."
"God is Infinite Wisdom, and Power, and Goodness—and Love—but if this idea is too vast for your human faculties if your mind loses itself in its overwhelming infinitude, fix it on Him who condescended to take our nature upon Him, who was raised to heaven even in his glorified human body, in whom the fullness of the godhead shines."

Nor is the reader spared the sordid descriptions of a progressively decaying body that inevitably accompanies moral corruption; or the terror of impending judgment.

Markham: Melodrama's Hero

Although Gilbert Markham, the gentleman farmer, gives the impression that he is virtuous, there are times when he, too, yields to physical violence and brutality. A few days after he had seen Helen walking with Lawrence, whom he believes to be her lover, by chance both men meet on horseback in an open field. Markham assaults his would-be rival for no reason. Lawrence falls to the ground, unconscious, Markham claps his spurs and gallops away. The voice of conscience, however, sends him back to help his rival, or to verify that he is still alive, but Lawrence, semiconscious now, refuses his aid and Markham leaves him to his own devices.

More complex than the paper-thin Huntingdon is Markham's blend of violence and prejudice combined with love and tenderness. He is not always honest, resorting, for example, to deception to learn Helen's true feelings about him. Nevertheless, he has clear ideas as to what is right and wrong, attempting even to enlighten Helen by providing suggestions for the education of her five-year-old son. Unaware of the difficulties she has had with an alcoholic husband, he accuses her of overreacting when she refuses to allow her son to drink the little glass of wine he offers him. She remonstrates that one glass can easily lead to a future vice—a theory upheld by modern medicine, which recognizes that the child of an alcoholic may inherit such a syndrome. Markham, however, maintains that to deny any and all liquor will only whet a child's appetite for the forbidden fruit. It will never make him virtuous.

Despite Markham's strong sexual attraction toward Helen, he, as so many heroes of melodrama, resists temptation. He acquiesces to all of her demands, even her interdict, after her widowhood, not to see her again. When he pleads with her, she changes her mind and tells him that they must neither see each other nor correspond for six months. With the patience of a saint and the dignity of a lord, he keeps his word: there is no contact between them until the time period has elapsed. When he hears by chance that Helen is engaged to another, his *rash* and *passionate* side takes over, compelling him to travel through deep snow by horse, foot, and gig, only to discover that the rumors were untrue. Finally, after one more try and a passionate outburst on Markham's part, Helen accepts his marriage proposal. Leaving the "lugubrious bonnet" worn by widows, she allows him to look at her "beautiful black hair unstinted still and unconcealed in its glossy luxuriance," after which he clasps "her to his heart in the instinctive dread of losing my new-found treasure." Like Agnes Grey, but after far more turmoil, the couple will find their happiness.

Gothic Ghosts

As in the Gothic writings of Ann Radcliffe—*The Romance of the Forest* (1791) and *Mysteries of Udolpho* (1794)—in which architectural constructs and landscape are used to create mood and a sense of mystery and suspense, so Anne uses similar techniques in her depiction of Wildfell Hall and its surroundings.

Built in the Elizabethan era, Wildfell Hall, on Helen's arrival, is in a state of decay. Made of dark gray stone, "venerable and picturesque... but, doubtless, cold and gloomy," its awesomeness sends chills up the reader's spine. Untended and untenanted for many a year, the weeds and grasses surrounding it heighten its fearsome countenance. Helen's neighbors are concerned for her safety: "ghostly legend and dark traditions... respecting the haunted hall and its departed occupants" abound.

Indeed, everything about Wildfell Hall is designed to generate sensations of malaise: the outside as well as the inside, with its "faded crimson cushion and lining which had been unpressed and unrenewed so many years, and the grim escutcheons, with their lugubrious borders of rusty black cloth."

In traditional, high-romantic style, Helen in her loneliness associates the setting sun with feelings of loss and bereavement, thus anticipating the gloom of things to come. In the morning, the outer world speaks another language. Birds sing their songs as they usher in a sense of abandon and renewal; the sea, like a pair of eyes, haunts, obsesses, and mesmerizes her.

In the preface to the second edition of *The Tenant*, Anne took an adamant stand castigating her critics overtly:

> I wish to tell the truth, for truth always conveys its own moral to those who are able to receive it. But as the *priceless treasure* too frequently hides at the bottom of a well, it needs some courage to dive for it, especially as he that does so will be likely to incur more scorn and obloquy for the mud and water into which he has ventured to plunge, than thanks for the jewel he procures.... Let it not be imagined, however, that I consider myself competent to reform the errors and abuses of society, but only that I would fain contribute my humble quota towards so good an aim, and if I can gain the public ear at all, I would rather whisper a few wholesome truths therein than much soft nonsense.

E. P. Whipple of the *North American Review* condemned *The Tenant* for the "prominence given to the brutal element of human nature," thus producing a lasting impression of "horror and disgust." James Lorrimer of the *North American Review* considered certain scenes detrimental to public morals, those "in which the author seems to pride himself on bringing his reader into the closest possible proximity with naked vice, and there are conversations such as we had hoped never to see printed in English." To such allegations, Anne wrote unflinchingly:

I find myself censured for depicting con amore, with "a morbid love of the coarse, if not the brutal" . . . when we have to do with vice and vicious characters, I maintain it is better to depict them as they really are than as they would wish to appear.[14]

Anne's ambition, as we know, was not to produce "a perfect work of art." Her goal was first and foremost evangelical: to teach what she believed to be the moral and loftly *lessons* of Christianity.

Audacious and courageous, Anne's heroines stand their ground, fight for the obligations of employers to respect and to pay their employee/governess a fair wage, for the right of a wife to keep her fortune in her own name and struggle against the financial dominance of a husband, for the abolition of lascivious and pernicious comportment, regarded as a sickness able to *contaminate* others, and for the rejection of the double standard.

Anne's unsentimental, skillfully built, and suspenseful scenes, the self-control in her writing, the smooth, ordered, classically constructed sentences, the subdued effects of rhetoric, and the insights into the psyches of her characters, drawn for the most part from observation were remarkable, given her age and experience. It is little wonder that George Moore again wrote: "If Anne Brontë had lived ten years longer she would have taken a place beside Jane Austen, perhaps even a higher place."[15]

4

Emily Brontë: Locked in One's Own World

> No coward soul is mine,
> No trembler in the world's storm-troubled sphere:
> I see Heaven's glories shine,
> And Faith Shines equal arming me from Fear.[1]

Emily's last poem, "No coward soul is mine," sums up not only her courageous views on life and death, but also her powerful faith in God, and equally powerful distaste for and rejection of organized religion. Confident in her beliefs, feelings, and identity she *knew* her way in life at a very early age.

Deeply introverted—more so than her sisters—Emily's rich and effulgent fantasy life fed by continuously pulsating subliminal contents was *her reality*. Unlike Anne's and Charlotte's protagonists, the unforgettable characters in *Wuthering Heights* were not intellectually conceived, even though the narrative structure was. Stamped with eternity and universality, the creatures conjured by Emily have been haunting and arousing readers for generations.

Emily, unlike her sisters, related instinctually to Mother Earth; she was viscerally connected to her moors in all of their manifestations. They fed her fantasy world, her body, and her psyche. Only at home, surrounded by *her* moors, did she find release from emotional bondage. Amid her natural surroundings she felt free to run recklessly or ramble carelessly through the immense wasteland, the boggy sedges and grasses, absorbing their ever-altering palette of colorful flowers and orchestrated bird songs. Exhilarated and strengthened by the variegated and dramatic configurations—rounded or arched hills, or sharp crevices and cliffs— each personified for her a feeling or thought, each spelled life in its never-ending levels.

Thrust upon her own resources, like her siblings, Emily also created a world of make-believe for herself. Naming the soldier

her brother had given her "Gravey," was symptomatic of her unreachable personality. Was he actually grave looking? Or did
Emily project her own serious, secretive, and withdrawn personality upon this figure? Was it through him that she would be able
to convey her chaotic subliminal realm? As had her sisters and
brother, she too created a world of islands and mainlands filled
with heroes and heroines, each dictating his or her personal needs
and desires in the kingdoms they ruled. "Emmii," as her siblings,
was also a "Genius," empowered to dictate the fate of her heroes
and heroines over life and death. At first, she went along on
Charlotte's and Branwell's expeditionary forays to the Northwest
coast of Africa, exploring and then conquering the Glass Town
Confederacy, renaming it Angria. When Charlotte left for Roe
Head School in 1831, Emily and Anne, perhaps liberated from
their elder sister's domination, struck out on their own, and created the Gondal sagas.

The inhabitants of Gondal, an island of moors and mountains
in the North Pacific, whose climate resembled that of Yorkshire,
colonized Gaaldine, an island in the South Pacific, endowed with
balmy breezes and an ever-blazing sun. Emily's pen flowed end-
lessly, in her world of heroes and heroines, amid violent battles,
raging seas, passionate love episodes, imprisonments, illnesses,
murders, harrowing events of all types common to the Byronic
and Gothic romantic traditions.

It was in February 1844 that Emily decided to divide her notebooks into two sections: the first, entitled "Gondal Poems," included forty-five poems; the second, untitled section, was made
up of thirty-one poems.

The Poems: "No Coward Soul Is Mine"

Emily's seemingly simple poems are deceptive. Obscure and coded,
they reveal an inner topography filled with chaos: a juxtaposition
of violence, hatred, heroism, pusillanimity, instinctuality, serenity,
passion, and rationalized refinements. Tennyson, the best-known
poet of the Victorian age, in his *Timbuctoo Poems, Chiefly Lyrical,* "The Lady of Shalott," "Morte d'Arthur," and *Idylls of the
King,* spoke forthrightly for the values of his time despite some
doubt as to the validity of its materialism and increasing scientific
pursuits. Emily's poetry, contrarily, came from the heart, but

divested of all maudlin and personal affectations. Nor was Emily one to experiment with form, as had Browning in his dramatic poem *Paracelsus,* his verse play, *Pippa Passes,* his monologues and soliloquies. Emily retained traditional stanzaic patterns, which afforded her greater ease in sounding out her spiritual and emotional needs.

Like Keats in his "Ode to a Nightingale" and "Autumn," Emily also turned for solace and strength to nature in all of its tints and tonalities, and its quiescent and turbulent moods. She took refuge from what she looked upon as a sordid present by leaping into a world of dream, without political or social intent nor interest in abstract thought. In keeping with Keatsian needs, as attested to in "La Belle Dame sans Merci" and "The Eve of St. Agnes," Emily's colors, imagery, and rhythmic interludes reflect an inner emotional climate, as well as a deeply receptive sensorial understanding of multiple facets of human experience.

Passion and melancholy sweep through Emily's verses as through Byron's. She too had his propensity for power, violence, and the fantastic, as evidenced in his *Childe Harold,* with its vigorous, moody, and defiant hero who, disillusioned with a life of pleasure, sets out on a solitary pilgrimage through Greece and Europe; in *The Giaour,* with its eerie and exotic concubine-heroine who escapes the clutches of Caliph Hassan; as in *The Prisoner of Chillon,* detailing the drama of François de Bonnivard, a sixteenth-century Genevan prelate, persecuted and imprisoned for his religious convictions; in *Manfred,* the mysterious, solitary, and defiant Faustian figure who sells his soul to the Prince of Darkness and lives thereafter divested of human feelings in splendid solitude in the Alps—and so many more powerfully romantic works that spawned Emily's imagination.

Emily, neither a poet of ideas nor an idealist, differed in this regard from the socially oriented Wordsworth and Shelley. She was not interested in bettering the standards of the populace, nor in furthering or retarding the growth of the industrial revolution, nor in social commentaries. Her poetry was metaphysical, pantheistic and passionate. Wedded to both the feeling and earthly domains, her writing was her lifeline to the world. Her verbal creations allowed her to commune with nature and people through the power of the imagination.

Essentially autobiographical, Emily's poems are paradoxically detached and collective in nature. The divestiture of everything that is private endows her work with singular strength and power, going beyond the visible and human domain. When writing about her lonely and distressing early years in "Come Hither, Child," she obliterates all familial incidents, thereby accentuating the haunting and obsessive nature of sorrow.

Although Emily's verses are traditional in form, her originality stems from the intensity of the passionate dramas she recounts. One of her most frequent themes is that of imprisonment, be it the soul captive within the body, the world of reason attempting to break out of its circumscribed realm into transpersonal spheres, or the rejection of all that stifles and crushes. She yearns for the freedom that would permit her to experience a unity between her soul and celestial spheres, yet she is also an earth person—tied, rooted, and viscerally connected to the land. When away from *her* moors and cloistered in a schoolroom or in someone's home, she ceases to exist as an individual, grows ill, and virtually withers. Like the Platonist, she seeks to escape into an incorruptible, perfect, transcendent sphere and is forever prevented from achieving her goal because of her human form: her flesh/body. Wedded to everything that grows, to the world of contingencies of life, she would gladly give up her earthly form for liberating death. The older she becomes, the greater grows her resentment of the limitations imposed upon her as a mortal. For her, liberty lies just on the other side of the visible and sensate world. Beatitude is known only after death.

To seek to live in the world of the imagination while divesting oneself of the mundane is, in a certain sense, to yearn for death (*thanatos*) in order to return to the fullness (*pleroma*) of God. For Emily, the existential sphere with all of its commitments, obligations, and commonplaces meant imprisonment in consciousness and in linear time, form, and matter. As infinite sadness settled into her life, she longed increasingly to cut herself off from any and all bonds, to sever herself from a world of entanglements. Emily's deathwish is no different from that of the German Romantic poet, Novalis, as conveyed in his six lyrical poems, *Hymns to the Night* (1800). As a geologist of the soul, each of his hymns cuts through layers of feeling in his desperate search for the mystical *center*, where the creative élan—or God—is experienced.

Like so many poets, including Racine, Goethe, and Baudelaire, Emily was torn by raging antagonistic powers within her being: black/white; earth/heaven; good/evil; love/hate, man/woman.

When swelling inner forces could no longer be contained, she resorted to Aristotelian catharsis, allowing her song to expel itself in violent, cruel, and explosive metaphors and images. Emily did not conform to the Platonic ideal of reason rising above subjective sorrows and discomfiture, nor did she reach that universal and abstract domain where timeless essences, forms, and ideas prevail. Intoxicated with feeling, she escaped via the word into the dream and, upon awakening to the world of reality, realized she was but a martyr, a captive of this earth. Hostage of her own limitations, she expended her energies, defying her condition in tempestuous, but also vulnerable stanzaic patterns. Verging from one extreme to the other, from joy and brilliant sun rays to the dismal hours of a sorrowful night, rarely, if ever, did she achieve balance or harmony.

Religious conflicts also characterized Emily's thematics. If she could rid herself of her logical and rational approach to Deity, she would be able to obliterate, she felt, the *Three Gods* of Christianity, thus enabling her to experience the Trinity as Unity. Only through the irrational or imaginative faculty could she perform such a feat. In the poem "To Imagination," Emily personified this single ruling principle, this force that had the power to release her from turmoil and sorrow. Like the French poet, Charles Baudelaire, who, a decade later, personified Imagination bowing with reverence to the "Queen of Faculties," so Emily, too, worshiped the dynamic force within her.

In a poignant apostrophe, Emily verbalized the feelings experienced as Imagination took flight, allowing her via, the dream, to inhabit ethereal spheres: "O Dream, where art thou now." Yearning for wholeness, she, who lived in the differentiated world of the rational human being, longed for oblivion, for the world beyond the limited sensate visible sphere, be it Heaven or Hell. Like the seer of old, Emily was forever attempting to extract herself from the shackles of contingency, and bathe, as in "My Comforter," in the purity of nonmaterial domains.

Reminiscent of the mystics of old—Heraclitus, Meister Eckhart, Giordano Bruno, Jakob Boehme—Emily viewed the energetic factor in the world in terms of relentless sequences of destruction and construction. Birth depends upon death because life feeds on the blood of others in its eternal round.

Emily's religious adventure into the world of death also took her into the subliminal spheres of proleptic dreams replete with prophetic encounters and erotic meanderings. As she leads her readers into chthonic regions or supernal spheres in the manner of a Dante, tonalities, each in turn together, pulsate stridently or mellifluously, taking on organic and inorganic form. Prodromal as well, Emily's verse is highly charged with sensations ranging from the searing of blazing coals to the sting of iced embers.

Emily rejected such Christian virtues as charity carried to the extreme, as embodied in Anne and Charlotte. Repudiating the tyranny of the *ought* or the *should,* she yearned for fulfillment, which she understood as the living out of her own directives and views in coordinated activities. That Emily escaped the obligatory Christian precepts in a home in which ethics were paramount is incredible.[2] She loved, but not out of obedience; she was kind, not because it was expected of her, but because she responded viscerally to all of God's creations, human, animal, or vegetal. Unlike many Christian thinkers who focus keenly on dogma that unites them with Christ, God, or the Holy Spirit, Emily sought to discover new spheres and fresh dimensions within and outside herself. Unlike her sisters who sought reform associated with good deeds, Emily understood that Evil could not be destroyed; she accepted it as implicit in the Godhead. As is written in Isaiah: "I form the light, and create darkness: I make peace, and create evil: I the Lord do all these things" (Isa. 45:7).

The question remains as to whether Emily *actually* did escape the tremendous burden of guilt and sin implicit in Christianity. Because she overtly disobeyed basic Christian precepts by rejecting organized religion, the burden of wrongdoing was far greater for her than for her sisters. Or had Emily merely repressed her feelings of guilt, allowing the energies in subliminal spheres to build to explosive force? How else could one account for that inner seething rage that emerged in those unforgettable characters who stalk the pages of *Wuthering Heights?*

Neither choosing the path of reason, nor indulging in discursive ways, Emily dug deep within her psyche to convey both her torment and her rapture, reverence and irreverence, love and hate, but always in terms of her fierce individuality. Direct experience allowed her to convey her awe and need of nature in her poems, and, in *Wuthering Heights,* such contact permitted her to be enraptured by the majesty of a tree, the myriad shadings of heather, the orchestration of nature's melodies, or the windswept rhythms of an ever-altering landscape. Her eye, instrument of perception, became her *inseeing* instrument able to penetrate the minutest detail in its general unfolding.

Pantheism absorbed Emily's being, animated her world, concretized the scenes she evoked, intensified cognition and lyricism, thus catalyzing her ecstatic hymnal songs with complex polyphonic modalities. In a poem purported to be her last—"No Coward soul is mine"—Emily had already succeeded in divesting herself of human limitations, joining cosmic forces taking her beyond the world of concretion. Emily Dickinson called her "gigantic Emily Brontë," and "No Coward soul is mine" was one of her favorite poems.[3]

Wuthering Heights: A Mythical Unfolding

Wuthering Heights is a myth—Emily's myth and her lifeline to the world. That the protagonists and the events narrated in *Wuthering Heights* stemmed from her archetypal depths endows the novel with timelessness and universality. Because of its mythical qualities, it is unfathomable, lending itself to multiple interpretations depending upon the depth of the reader's projection. Understandably, *Wuthering Heights* both repelled and terrified, gripped and fascinated, the author's contemporaries. While the evils recounted transgressed the puritanical cultural canon of Emily's day, its great love motif haunted and mesmerized, then even as today.

A myth—the narration of a not necessarily personal but transcendental primordial experience—is not something invented for the sake of entertainment. Although it may also be diverting or engaging, it is, rather, a living and burning reality that exists in the psyche and culture of an individual and a people. A myth deals with both the existential world and the internal experiences, thus with both temporal and atemporal matters.

Because a myth lives outside temporal time, events and characters in *Wuthering Heights* are not bound by the limits of linear or historical time, flowing instead in a cyclical, sacred, or eternal dimension. Myth time in Emily's novel is reversible: it includes both a twenty-four-hour cycle, flashbacks, and an atemporal dream time, taking events out of a present to a moment in the past and back again. Happenings can occur and reoccur; they can seem credible or implausible.

Myths of many nations are replete with searing love experiences that either lead to union after death or redemption upon completion of certain heroic tasks. Examples in literature are "Cupid and Psyche," "Orpheus and Euridice," *Tristan and Isolde, The Dybbuk, Pelléas and Mélisande,* "Annabel Lee," and *Wuthering Heights* as well. It narrates, over a span of two generations, the vicissitudes of two couples, Catherine and Heathcliff, unearthly lovers who are doomed to living out their passion only after death; the second, Catherine and Hareton, rooted in everyday reality, can cope with the difficult events confronting them, and are able to live out the fulfillment of their destiny.

The central theme in *Wuthering Heights* is the birth, burgeoning, and death of love on a worldly plane, and the rebirth of this passion in atemporal spheres. Love, or Eros, understood philosophically, not only represents the attraction one person feels for another, but also symbolizes a unifying force in nature. The myth of Eros (relatedness) and his brother Anteros (the Greek God of unrequited love, overcome with bitterness and anguish, who seeks revenge and is known as the agent of discord and dismemberer of all that is linked in the cosmos) may be applied to Catherine and Heathcliff. Accordingly, there are periods in *Wuthering Heights,* and in history as well, when Eros prevails and other times when Anteros reigns.

Catherine is doomed from the very outset never to know earthly joy. Identifiable with the Alexandrian saint Catherine who was martyred by decapitation after which angels carried her body to Mt. Sinai for her mystical marriage with Christ, so Catherine would experience her marriage only after her release from the limitations of worldly existence. During her life, she was wedded to Heathcliff only through the medium of nature, considered by both as a living, breathing, sustaining, or death-dealing organism. This very name, Heathcliff, suggests a combination of elemental forces: *heath* (a tract of uncultivated land, rich in peat, heather, and small flowers and plants), and *cliff* (steep overhanging rock, precipice), an indication of the dangers to be encountered by undirected and instinctive existence.

The House or Temenos

That the archetypal Catherine and Heathcliff should live out their passion within a *temenos* or sacred space—two houses, Wuthering

Heights and Thrushcross Grange, and the moors—is suitable. In ancient times sanctuaries or *temeni* were built to enable mortals to reach up to their Gods, thereby allowing and encouraging an intimacy between human and divine spheres.

The very definition of the word *wuthering* may be viewed as a premonitory indication of the mysterious happenings to be experienced by those inhabiting the edifice. A provincial adjective signifying "atmospheric tumult," such as stormy weather, the word is a mirror image of the emotional climate in the building and its occupants. Although Wuthering Heights stands high on a hill (closeness to the sun implied), the protagonists are, paradoxically, associated with dark, cold, starkness, and evil. While Thrushcross Grange, larger and more comfortably furnished and situated on lower ground, is associated with light and warmth. Polarities are in place from the very outset.

Wuthering Heights, built in 1500, suffers from a kind of malnutrition: its thorns have become barren, its firs stunted, everything seems to crave for the "alms of the sun" that sustain life. The mobility of the elements associated with Wuthering Heights are evident in such words as *wind,* representing the spirit and breath of God (when He breathed "a living soul" into Adam [Gen. 2:7]). The wind blustering about the *temenos* transports, metaphorically speaking, Catherine and Heathcliff into another dimension.

Wuthering Heights and Heathcliff as well were built to withstand the vagaries of nature. The author's use of parallel personifications to depict specific parts of the house as analogous to Heathcliff's face reveal stunning insights into his character: "narrow windows are deeply set in the wall, and the corners defended with large jutting stones" may be juxtaposed to Heathcliff's "black eyes withdrawn so suspiciously under their brows." Other details suggest the secrecy within this powerfully structured, but fearfully tenebrous home, decorated by a "quantity of grotesque carvings," along with "a wilderness of crumbling griffins and shameless little boys" over the front of the main door of Wuthering Heights. The griffin, a fabulous animal identified in medieval times with the eagle and the lion, symbolizes both heavenly and earthly forces: Christ and Satan. Of Persian and Zoroastrian origin, the griffin represented primordial warring principles—Good and Evil—the very fundaments of life. Within the cloistered walls of Wuthering Heights, then, life may be viewed as a continuous shifting between two polarities.

Wuthering Heights is patriarchal and primitive. Stark in its bareness, ascetic in its layout, unfriendly in its appearance, its lack of conviviality and warmth is augmented by stone floors, "villainous old guns," "horse-pistols" placed above the chimney, and "a hive" of half a dozen sheep dogs ready to assault any unwanted visitor. The only feminine element present is a "liver-coloured bitch pointer, surrounded by a swarm of squealing puppies."

Thrushcross Grange is a matriarchal seat, where live the Lintons and their children, Edgar and Isabella. Unlike Wuthering Heights, it is elegant and comfortable—"a splendid place carpeted with crimson, and crimson covered chairs and tables, and a pure white ceiling bordered by gold, a shower of glass-drops hanging in silver chains from the centre, and shimmering with little soft tapers." Sunlight streams into the home through the large windows, permitting communication between outer and inner worlds.

Premonitory Dreams

The stranger from the south of England, Mr. Lockwood, arriving in Yorkshire on a misty, cold, and snowy night, is the catalytic agent who sets the action in motion. Lockwood, the new tenant at Thrushcross Grange, cannot reach his destination because of bad weather and must remain the night at Wuthering Heights. Without Heathcliff's knowledge, the housekeeper shows him into an ice-cold bedroom that has remained unoccupied for the past twenty years—that of the deceased Catherine Earnshaw. Before retiring, Lockwood reads some of Catherine's thirty-year-old diary and "a pious discourse delivered by the Rev. Jabes Branderham," before sinking into a deep sleep during which he dreams the following:

Old Joseph, the handyman at Wuthering Heights, is guiding Lockwood through the snow to a chapel, which he enters. There, he listens to Reverend Branderham's incredibly long and dull sermon on sinfulness: "Seventy Times Seven" divided into 490 parts, each devoted to a separate sin. (Matt. 18:21–22). Upon reaching the Seventy-First sin, Lockwood is angered by the vacuousness of the preachings and intends to denounce him "as the sinner of the sin that no Christian need pardon." Instead, the preacher accuses Lockwood of the same sin, singles him out for chastisement, and calls upon the worshipers to rush toward him with clubs or fists and strike him—which they do. "Every man's hand was against his neighbor."

That Joseph, a religious fanatic, is Lockwood's guide, indicates not only the spread of such malignant values, but the destructiveness of evangelicalism and sermonizing. Rather than arouse love, they spell hatred and stir the worst instincts in human nature. Lockwood is so disturbed by the fracas heard in his dream that he awakens, tries to rationalize its cause, and ascribes his fright to the fir-tree brushing against the window panes during the snowstorm. Nevertheless, his unconscious remains unsatisfied by this explanation and, to draw attention to the problem at stake, sends him a "frightful nightmare."

In the second dream, Lockwood actually hears a fir-bough rubbing against the windowpane. Unable to unhasp the casement, he thrusts his knuckles through the glass, stretches his arm out to seize the branch, but instead his fingers close on "a little, ice-cold hand!" Horrified, he tries to withdraw his arm, but the hand clings to him. He hears a voice sobbing: "Let me in—let me in!" He asks who it is. "Catherine Linton . . . I'm come home: I'd lost my way on the moor!" Lockwood sees the face of a child looking through the window. Terrified, he pulls the little wrist down onto the broken pane, rubbing it to and fro until the blood runs down. "Begone!" he shouts. "I'll never let you in, not if you beg for twenty years." The voice mourned: "It is twenty years . . . twenty years. I've been a waif for twenty years!" So terrified is Lockwood that he screams in his sleep, awakening Heathcliff, who enters the bedroom.

The nightmare is complex and may be analyzed in terms of its specific images. That the little girl holds onto Lockwood's *hand* symbolizes an outward manifestation of an inner attitude or an overt act of solidarity and supplication between two virtually lifeless beings: the dead girl and the emotionally dead Lockwood lying in his coffinlike oak closet bed. Iconographically, the hand represents a uniting principle, injecting energy from one bloodless and ice-cold being to another. To open Lockwood—or the *locked wood*—to the dead feminine principle is Catherine's goal. Reminiscent of certain Medieval tombs in which a hand is extended outside the coffin in an attempt to grasp and then force the passerby to join the dead in the other world, the pleading-hand image may be viewed as a paradigm of Lockwood's fear of the unknown, the irrational, everything that cannot be explained, the very death/life mystery.

The child's face seen outside the pane of glass by Lockwood is a mirror image of his own stressful, unsettled, and distorted formative years. To dream about a child image usually precedes some psychological change. In that the primordial image of the child represents both unity and plurality, the beginning and the end, pre- and postconsciousness, it suggests the spontaneous manifestation of an undeveloped factor emerging in Lockwood's *locked wooden* psyche. That Lockwood rubbed the child's hand against the broken pane, thus drawing blood in what some critics termed a sadistic act, not only reveals the depth of Lockwood's wound as a child, but the agony he must experience if transformation is to come about. Blood spells death as well as life.

The image of the window, used multiple times in *Wuthering Heights,* is to the house what eyes are to the body: a means of looking out into the world, onto the unknown. It symbolizes separation between the outer universe and the closed, circumscribed, static, and decaying existence within the house. Until Lockwood breaks the glass there can be, symbolically speaking, no interaction between outer and inner worlds, each cut off from the other by means of some opaque substance, some moral, psychological, or spiritual interdict. Before the breaking of the glass, no integration of opposites has occurred. The shattering of this hard, cutting, and bruising substance serves as a rite of passage, requiring some brutal act, such as the shedding of blood, to energize the growth process.

The little girl attempting to enter the window may be identified with a soul image or *anima* figure—an autonomous psychic content in the male personality, which establishes emotional and sexual relationship with the opposite sex. Lockwood's connection with women has not gone beyond the infantile stage and will not, as long as he remains cut off from his anima. He relates the incident of having been in love with a "most fascinating creature, a real goddess" with whom he remained in love "as long as she took no notice" of him. The minute she expressed attachment to him, he tired: "I confess it with shame—shrunk icily into myself, like a snail; at every glance retired colder and farther" away. The word *icily* underscores the identification between his love experience and the ice-cold hand of the child, which he rejects, and forcing the child to remain outside the house.

The child in Lockwood's nightmare, referred to by some as a ghost, may be viewed as an unconscious content that, unless brought into consciousness, cannot be redeemed. Ghosts or apparitions, considered disembodied spirits, are, psychologically, primordial forms of the autonomous image-creating activity of the unconscious, and may spell some form of psychic dissociation.[4] That Lockwood was haunted by a ghost suggests that his overly rational view of life had led to a fundamental imbalance in his psyche. The repression of what is unknowable is an attempt on his part to annihilate those unfathomable contents living inchoate in his collective unconscious. The ghost of the dead little girl represented what he feared: his deeply maimed and until now rejected anima, which lay dormant in his psyche and which had to be awakened and revivified if he were to function harmoniously in life. The French word for ghost, *revenant,* from the verb "to return" (*revenir*), conveys the idea that until the psyche is satisfied with itself, its image-making power will return over and over again in different shapes and forms to show its pain or distaste until the individual awakens to what is missing or repressed.

Lockwood's role—that of the outsider—is to unravel the mystery revealed to him by his dream. Upon leaving the following morning for Thrushcross Grange he will begin to fulfill his destiny. It is there that he meets Nelly Dean, the housekeeper, once the nurse of Catherine (Linton, née Earnshaw), therefore emotionally involved in the events to be narrated. Like the chorus in ancient Greek theater, Nelly will both reveal the events and participate in them. At times, she is a protective force; at other instances, a betrayer of confidences, catalyzing the conflicts necessary to effect transformation. The active role played by Nelly throughout the narrative is instrumental in bringing the two families—the Earnshaws and the Lintons—together, thereby bringing harmony and balance out of chaos.

The Love Duet

Although Lockwood arrives at Wuthering Heights in 1801, the events Nelly is to narrate span a thirty-year period. A regression into the "beginning" or childhood projects the reader into a timeless period, thus transforming profane into transcendent space, and concrete events into atemporal ones. Struggles serve to test the mettle of the protagonists and to arouse duality, bringing awareness of both sides of a situation and leading to expanded consciousness.[5]

In the "beginning," happiness reigned at Wuthering Heights. Hindley and Catherine Earnshaw and their parents were, seemingly, a felicitous unit. One day, for reasons unknown, Mr. Earnshaw takes a sixty-mile walk to Liverpool and back again. Before leaving, he asks his children what presents he should bring back to them. Hindley asks for a fiddle; Catherine—a fine equestrian though barely six years old—a whip. The gifts in themselves are paradigms of the characters; the violin represents music and the *feeling* world; the whip suggests punishment and brutality, but is also a symbol of power and an attribute of the Terrible Earth Mother.

On Mr. Earnshaw's return, Hindley becomes angry because the violin has been smashed. His feelings, we may suggest, have been crushed, auguring a destruction of the connecting principle between him and his father. The whip, lost en route, divests Catherine for the moment of her latent cruelty, dominating manner, and capacity for bloodletting. The kindly Mr. Earnshaw did not, however, return empty-handed. He brought the family another and most unwanted present, which he called "a gift of God; though it's as dark almost as if it came from the devil."

What was *it*? "A dirty, ragged, black-haired child" or, as Mrs. Earnshaw referred to him, a "gypsy brat" she wanted to eject. Old Mr. Earnshaw, in keeping with his religious principles, had taken pity on this homeless and starving boy found in the streets. Bringing him home, he asked his wife to wash him, give him clothes, and put him to sleep with their own children, which aroused the entire family's anger. Hindley and Catherine refused to have "it" sleep with them; Nelly, acquiescing to the childrens' demands put "it" on the stair landing, hoping "it" might be gone on the morrow." Instead, "it" crept to Mr. Earnshaw's door, the only member of the family that had shown "it" warmth and tenderness. Nelly, punished for her inhumanity, was banished from the house for a few days.

That "it" was christened "Heathcliff"—named after an Earnshaw son who had died in childhood—not only suggests how partial Mr. Earnshaw was to this newcomer, but how deep was the mysterious bond between the two. After Heathcliff's arrival, the family relationships changed drastically: Cathy and Heathcliff took such a liking to each other that they became virtually inseparable. No longer the outsider, the reject, the hateful "usurper," as Hindley called him, Heathcliff became the focus of Cathy's and Mr. Earnshaw's tenderness. Hindley, on the other hand, was transformed into the unwanted third. Mrs. Earnshaw, unsolicitous of the newcomer, never helped him when she saw him wronged.

Heathcliff, found in Liverpool, or the "pool of life," is the hero or antihero of *Wuthering Heights:* the harbinger of the new, the different, those factors tradition seeks to shut out because of the possibly fearsome and chaotic nature of such unknown quantities. Yet, this is the very nourishment that makes for future growth. Unlike some solar heroes, such as Achilles, Roland, Siegfried, and Parzival, Heathcliff works in darkness and murky realms. He is like the seed that feeds on nutrients buried deep within Mother Earth until such time as germination occurs, after which time it develops strength enough to burst through the soil's crust, thus breaking asunder what is whole.

Heathcliff is, psychologically speaking, the paradigm of the ego (center of consciousness) attempting to wrench itself free from a stunted family situation. Considered Evil, in his capacity as disrupter, causing pain and dissension within the status quo, he may be viewed as the harbinger of increased consciousness.

In keeping with the structure of ancient myths, as long as the Old King—in our case, Old Mr. Earnshaw—is alive, Heathcliff blooms, thriving under paternal warmth, generosity, and solicitude. Yet, even at this early stage, some of his unpleasant characteristics emerge: he becomes spoiled, deceitful, power-hungry, and is unsparing in his cruelty against his enemy, Hindley.

Orphans and strangers, like Adam and Eve after they were cast from paradise, are those who have been cut off from family, environment, and themselves. According to St. Augustine, they took on the function of the pilgrim, understood symbolically as a potential rival or messenger of either God or the Devil. Both orphan and stranger must be received with warmth if a psychic reconciliation and integration is to be effected. Heathcliff, a being who lives at the edge of two worlds, represents an unknown and nameless dynamic that makes for transformation.

What compelled Mr. Earnshaw to bring home a dirty waif? Was he trying to live the fundaments of ancient Christianity, Christ's Word having grown arid and His thought ossified? Had the Earnshaw family become complacent in their joyous bliss? and nonconscious paradisaic state of uncommitted childhood? Had they sought to cut themselves off from the outside world, seeking to retain their pristine purity, so antithetical to the life process? Was their intent to reject anything that might change or alter their static well-being?

That Mr. Earnshaw had called Heathcliff a "gift of God" suggests the importance he gave to the integration of Evil and Good, Light and Dark, no matter what the price. Like Satan or Lucifer

(Latin *fiat lux*, bring light), Heathcliff would spread chaos, but in so doing, would be the bearer of eventual enlightenment. In keeping with ancient mythic structures, transformation began the moment Mr. Earnshaw started favoring and spoiling Heathcliff and denigrating his own son. Jealousy and rancor reached such intensity—Hindley growing uncontrollably irascible—that life at Wuthering Heights became unbearable. Hindley was sent away to school—cast out of the home—while Heathcliff, the former stranger, took his place as the father's beloved son. Although, as in ancient times, the black sheep was sent away to rectify an evil within the community, believing that all would be well after his disappearance, such simplistic views would never come to pass in the Earnshaw family.

After Mr. and Mrs. Earnshaw's death, and Hindley's return to Wuthering Heights with a secretly married and adored wife, Heathcliff begins his martyrdom. With no protective patriarchal power to stem the tide of Hindley's corrosive rage, Heathcliff once again becomes the pariah. He is relegated to the stables, deprived of education, and treated like a subhuman. Although repressing his hatred in order to survive, there were moments when his feelings were charged with uncontrollable affects, reaching explosive force as in the form of "black tempers."

Heathcliff, like his prototypes Satan and Lucifer, was complex: "sullen" but patient, "hardened by ill-treatment," quiet and "insensible." A stoic of sorts, he withstood Hindley's persecutions and beatings without shedding a tear or uttering a word of complaint, which might imply defeat on his part.

Catherine, Heathcliff's constant companion, is depicted as a "wild, wicked slip," a bold and saucy mischief maker who sang, and laughed and plagued everyone with her willful manner. She held the psychological *whip*—the prototype of the one her father had lost en route from Liverpool—not hesitating to use it, for example to ridicule Joseph's religious curses. She permitted herself all license and all spontaneity, without ever thinking about the consequences of her acts. Undeveloped, with no sense of commitment or thought for the feelings of others, she was somewhat like Epimetheus (Greek, afterthought), reacting after the damage had been done. As an archetypal earth force, her great joy lay in roaming the moors with Heathcliff—freely and in utter abandon. Psychologists might identify the moors with the Great Mother—vegetal life in its primeval state. Its multitude of grasses and flowers might disorient the uninitiated, but not Catherine and Heathcliff, who knew and treasured each of the Great Mother's outgrowths, and particularly the purplish pink heather.

As an offspring of the Great Mother, Catherine dictated to Heathcliff, her slave who yielded to her every wish and desire with uncompromising and eternal love. As a dominant power, it was she who invaded his soul. They became *one*, although double in their fatal love duet.

Paradise Shattered

The Serpent that caused the fall of Adam and Eve from, psychologically speaking, a nonconscious state in the Garden of Eden to consciousness on Earth, reappears in *Wuthering Heights* and is instrumental in precipitating Catherine and Heathcliff's sudden exile from their paradisaic realm of childhood. Hindley, as the new master of Wuthering Heights, meted out punishment to Catherine and Heathcliff by relegating them to the cold washhouse. Unwilling to accept imprisonment, Heathcliff suggested to Catherine that they slip out for a run on the moors despite the rain. Their *escape* and their reckless *escapade* consisted of racing each other, the shod Heathcliff beating the barefooted Catherine. Their venturesome course had taken them inadvertently to the elegant Linton home, Thrushcross Grange. Never having seen it at close range, they were curious to see more. Planting themselves on a flowerpot under the drawing-room window, they peered into the Lintons' lighted elegant drawing room. Edgar and his sister, Isabella, were alone. Catherine and Heathcliff's expectancy was that they should be happy, but the eleven-year-old Isabella, a year younger than Catherine, "lay screaming at the farther end of the room," while "Edgar stood on the hearth weeping silently, and in the middle of the table sat a little dog, shaking its paw and yelping." They had evidently been quarreling over the little dog, each pulling at him in different directions. "The idiots!" Heathcliff exclaimed and he and Catherine laughed, causing the frightened Linton children to scream for their mama and their papa. Fearing chastisement for trespassing on private property, Heathcliff and Catherine attempted to run away but the loosened bulldog bit Catherine, who was brought into the house and ministered to while Heathcliff—the "gypsy," the heathen, the "wicked boy"—was deprecated and forced out by the Linton family. Meanwhile,

Catherine's feet were bathed, she was given slippers, her beautiful hair was combed, she was offered cakes, and, in the end, she remained at the Lintons for five weeks, while Heathcliff resumed his pariahlike existence at Wuthering Heights.

Nature has a strange way of coming to the aid of those who seek, unconsciously or otherwise, to evolve out of an unregenerate childhood condition. The five-week stay at the grange served to transform Catherine. Her return to Wuthering Heights on Christmas Eve may be associated, psychologically, with the burgeoning of a new attitude toward life (the birth of the ego out of the self). Her resulting increased consciousness also signifies her ejection from paradise (her world of childhood and noncommitment) and entry into a domain of choice (differentiation). No longer living in wonder and *oneness* with Heathcliff, a new ruling principle emerges. Catherine has become cognizant of that *other* side of life—gracious living—represented by the Lintons of Thrushcross Grange. Henceforth, her worlds will be polarized and conflicted, causing uncertainty to prevail.

The changed Catherine has superimposed upon the former little girl running barefoot and recklessly through the savage moors a new persona or public face—the one society expects from those who seek to please and to attract others to their orbit. Previously, only Catherine's instinctive and earthy side had been functional. During her five-week stay at the Lintons, she was taught manners, wore fine clothes, and learned to flatter others, thereby winning everyone's affection, including Edgar's. Two personalities now dwelled in her: the primitive childlike creature, and the social young lady ready to approach marriage and perhaps even motherhood. Catherine delighted in her new persona and was pleased when Hindley commented: "You look like a lady now." Had the polarities—the instinctive little girl and the socially oriented beauteous woman—been integrated, harmony rather than turmoil would have dominated her personality.

Although Catherine kissed Heathcliff upon her return to Wuthering Heights, she could not help but comment on his appearance: "Why, how very black and cross you look!" she said. Heathcliff, shamed, his pride cut, reacted predictably—that is, aggressively: "I shall not stand to be laughed at ... I shall be as dirty as I please: and I like to be dirty, and I will be dirty." Dirt versus cleanliness, emphasized throughout the novel, represents a basic antagonism that was not overt as long as Catherine and

Heathcliff lived in a primal identification with nature. Now that she had opted for elegance, refinement, and artifice, she was no longer able to play out her role as Heathcliff's twin. Heathcliff is humiliated by the cruelty of Catherine's remarks. The single person in the world whose love and companionship he had enjoyed and depended upon in an environment of extreme emotional deprivation has now abandoned him. Devastated by the loss, the void within his psyche triggers latent patterns of behavior—cruelty, revenge, brutality, boorishness in actions and language, and uncontrollable rages—as means of self-defense.

Looking upon the new Catherine with terror, Heathcliff feels displaced by her different comportment, isolated, unprotected, and deeply alone. Unable to cope with his intense feelings of rejection, he withdraws still further into himself. Refusing to eat, he draws away from humans altogether, remaining in the stable where he spends his time tending the animals or returning to the moors. Heathcliff's self-imposed isolation activates his libido (psychic energy), stirring latent contents in his unconscious. Shifts in viewpoints may occur under such circumstances, as, for example, the change in the Hebrews after their exile from Egypt and their forty-year wanderings in the desert; and to Christ, after his forty-day stay in the desert. The moors used to activate dormant energies in Heathcliff and in Catherine, enabling them to throw off the morbid atmosphere prevailing at home. Their personification of plants and birds encouraged them to create a society of animate beings, thereby orchestrating a whole feeling realm. The joy that such fantasy life brought them enabled them to grapple with their own dissatisfactions and loveless world at Wuthering Heights. Identified with the primitive level of the psyche, the moors acted as a protective maternal shelter, holding both Heathcliff and Catherine in a kind of psychologically incestuous thrall.

Following Heathcliff's period of withdrawal into the animal and vegetal world after Catherine's return from Thrushcross Grange, he went through a transformation, at least on the surface. "Nelly, make me decent," he said, "I'm going to be good." She complied, but not without telling him that he had "grieved" Catherine and had made her cry. Heathcliff also admits crying. Although Nelly admonishes him for his pride, which invites sorrow, she also bolsters his self-confidence by telling him that he is stronger, younger, taller than Edgar Linton. If only, he answers, he had "light hair and fair skin," "and was dressed and behaved as well, and had a chance of being as rich as he will be."

The words *grief, grieve,* and *grave* are keys to an understanding of the archetypal Heathcliff and Catherine, both of whom are identified with sorrow. Although the former feels it more acutely than the latter, they are and will, henceforth, mourn their childhood—a past that can no longer be recaptured, replete with nonawareness and noncommitment, which cannot be carried into the next stage of psychological development: adulthood.

Nelly, Heathcliff's advisor and friend, warns him that to bemoan his fate—not having "light hair and fair skin"—is not only to no avail, but is a mark of self-indulgence. Heathcliff must, she maintains, look into the outer world and not remain obsessed with and imprisoned in his misery.

Change is in the offing for Heathcliff. That he now realizes he can never have Edgar Linton's "great blue eyes and even forehead" is a step forward. That he reasons sufficiently to compare himself with another and to understand that there are elements within his reach and others that are not, indicates the birth of a new attitude. He had attained the point of *questioning* himself concerning a new life orientation. Like Parzival, Heathcliff will have to *quest* for his grail. He will have to learn to synthesize conscious and unconscious contents, to give his life focus and a center, bringing balance and harmony to an area of chaos. To succeed in his endeavor, Heathcliff would also have to ask the *question* that Parzival had failed to ask the first time, but succeeded in asking the second, thereby successfully accomplishing his mission.

Heathcliff was ready to take the first step forward: he bathed, changed his clothes, and combed his hair. Nelly was so pleased with the results and thought this *new* lad so handsome that she wondered whether he might not be the kidnaped son of a Chinese emperor and an Indian queen. Were he to be restored to his parents, he would be able to buy Wuthering Heights and Thrushcross Grange with one week's income.

Nelly's fantasizing about his possible origin, reminiscent of Parzival, who was unaware of his heritage until he was well on the road to maturity, opens unlimited horizons to Heathcliff. But like other heroes—Cuchulainn or Heracles—Heathcliff must prove his worth by accomplishing extraordinary exploits. Unenlightened sybaritic brawn is not sufficient to win battles in the world of adults. Odyssean ruse and strategy are crucial if he is to achieve his goals.

His first ordeal will be to conquer the world of continuous humiliation and punishment meted out by Hindley. The death of Hindley's beloved wife from consumption after the birth of their son, Hareton, had filled him with rage against God and humankind—certainly increasing his fiendishness toward Heathcliff. His drunkenness and dissipation involve sadistic acts, which he perpetrates against his enemy of long-standing, Heathcliff. Biding his time, Heathcliff does not forget such outrage. "I am trying to settle how I shall pay Hindley back," no matter how long it takes, he tells Nelly.

Catherine, observing the abuse heaped upon Heathcliff by her brother, shows a lack of compassion and sympathy. As her animus figure, Heathcliff symbolizes the scared and distorted unconscious masculine contrasexual elements within her psyche. With only her new persona in mind, she compares Heathcliff's dark and uncouth ways and lack of education to Edgar's light, elegant, and knowledgeable manners. Glitter attracts her; marriage to the future owner of the grange is more to her liking than remaining in the primitive and unpleasant world identified with Wuthering Heights.

Yet, not everything is simple for Catherine. Although yearning for beauty and gracious living, she is not yet ready to give up her wild and impulsive ways as "queen of the countryside... a haughty headstrong creature!" Furthermore, as the anima figure of both Heathcliff and Edgar, she thrives on their adulation and love.[6] They are votaries for her: two men are at her feet, and she possesses complete power over both. That whip she had wanted her father to bring back to her from Liverpool is now at her disposal, to use as she pleases.

Cruelty is crucial in whipping people into place and Catherine is not adverse to using any means to gain her end. Never having developed any thinking faculty and completely self-indulgent, she is oblivious to the sorrow she inflicts on others. Her lack of discernment and her inability or unwillingness to distinguish right from wrong, encourages her to act impulsively, in typical childlike manner and in complete disregard of others. She can fit into two environments: she has learned to play expertly at being the refined lady capable of entertaining the most elegant of people; she can also be the tomboy running barefoot through the moors. But she no longer feels comfortable in either role. Because each side of her personality is incompatible with the other, she sees the chasm between her new self and Heathcliff as impossible to bridge.

After witnessing one of Hindley's abominations during his maniacal drunken orgies, the twenty-two-year-old and essentially schizoid Catherine decides to marry Edgar, although she knows she shall live to regret it: "In my soul and in my heart, I'm convinced I'm wrong. Nelly, I *am* Heathcliff." Catherine's double personality is controllable so long as no obstacles stand in her way. If she is thwarted in any manner, balance is destroyed and her repressed subliminal contents—those unregenerate monstrous forces buried deep within her collective unconscious—explode.

Catherine's proleptic dream in which she finds herself in heaven, reveals her deeply troubled state.

I was only going to say that heaven did not seem to be my home; and I broke my heart with weeping to come back to earth; and the angels were so angry that they flung me out into the middle of the heath on the top of Wuthering Heights; where I woke sobbing for joy. That will do to explain my secret, as well as the other. I've no more business to marry Edgar Linton than I have to be in heaven; and if the wicked man in there had not brought Heathcliff so low, I shouldn't have thought of it. It would degrade me to marry Heathcliff now; so he shall never know how I love him: and that, not because he's handsome, Nelly, but because he's more myself than I am. Whatever our souls are made of his and mine are the same; and Linton's is as different as a moonbeam from lightning, or frost from fire.

No sooner had Catherine said, "It would degrade me to marry Heathcliff," than Nelly notices a shadow rising from the bench in the next room and stealing out. It was Heathcliff. He never heard the end of Catherine's sentence that conveyed her love for him.

When Nelly asks her whether she has thought about how she will bear being separated from Heathcliff and "how he'll bear to be quite deserted in the world" Catherine is so deeply involved in her own world that she does not even understand the meaning of Nelly's question. Nor does she understand the commitments involved in marriage. Edgar will be taught to like Heathcliff, she informs Nelly, for she has no intention of ever giving him up. In fact, her husband's money will help Heathcliff make something of himself. Nelly, however, is quick to point out the unrealistic nature of her ideas. Nothing, Catherine maintains, will change.

If all else perished, and *he* remained, I should still continue to be; and if all else remained, and he were annihilated, the universe would turn to a mighty stranger: I should not seem a part of it. My love for Linton is like the foliage in the woods: time will change it, I'm well aware, as winter changes the trees. My love for Heathcliff resembles the eternal rocks beneath: a source of little visible delight, but necessary. Nelly, I *am* Heathcliff! He's always, always in my mind: not as a pleasure, any more than I am always a pleasure to myself, but as my own being.

Catherine's identification of Edgar with trees, their foliage undergoing seasonal change, suggests the fragility of the persona she had donned upon returning from her stay at Thrushcross Grange. That Heathcliff is associated with a rock indicates the power he represents within her. He is the steady, solid, long-lasting fundament of her being, her identity, her very life.

When Nelly informs Catherine that Heathcliff might have heard a good part of what she said, she looks frantically about for him, then screams out: "I want to speak to him, and I *must*, before I go upstairs." When she discovers that he is nowhere about, she is desperate and runs out in the storm searching for Heathcliff who had long since gone. Unable to cope with the divestiture of the deepest part of herself—the price she must pay for choosing to marry exogamously—Catherine falls victim to a dangerous illness. The doctor warns that "she would not bear crossing much; she ought to have her own way; and it was nothing less than murder in her eyes for any one to presume to stand up and contradict her."

Learning of Catherine's illness, Mrs. Linton took her to the Grange to nurse her, but soon after her recovery, Mr. and Mrs. Linton die from the fever transmitted to them. Catherine marries Edgar and lives, together with his sister, Isabella, at the grange.

What was the nature of Catherine's sickness, which made her suffer an eclipse of her ego or consciousness, leaving her even more ill at ease and disturbed with herself than before? Her condition of emotional stress was so powerful now that the "rock"—Heathcliff—was no longer present to steady and contain her feelings. Irrationality caused Catherine to fly into uncontrollable rages. The volatility of her unstable inner world and her hyperemotionalism indicated that she was under the dominion of unpredictable unconscious forces.

Catherine is now psychologically split. As long as she had been able to remain the little girl, the adolescent, answerable only to herself and Heathcliff, equilibrium was maintained. No demands were made upon her on a personal level. Once she became Edgar's wife, the responsibilities of marriage shattered the balance. With an enfeebled ego, further depleted after Heathcliff's departure, cut off from that darkened realm within her subliminal sphere that she had inhabited, Catherine became half a being, forced to live and fit into a confining persona. With the breakdown of relationship between fantasy and reality came a redistribution of values with which she could cope, but only when she was not thwarted. Even then, she experienced periods of intermittent depression and petulance. After Catherine's marriage to Edgar, he and Isabella, rather than risk Catherine's explosions, chose to remain silent.

Heathcliff's fate was also devastating. Upon hearing Catherine's deprecating remarks about him, he left Wuthering Heights. Prior to his departure, however, sensing separation to be imminent, he separated himself still further than before from his surroundings, taking on the traits of an autistic personality, his thinking becoming increasingly subjective and obsessive. When faced with objective events, he always gave them subjective intent and significance. Because everything he thought and felt emanated from his unconscious, the content of his thoughts and feelings became endogenous. Heathcliff's autistic temperament was evident in his behavioral patterns since his arrival at Wuthering Heights; covert in response to Mr. Earnshaw's kindness; after his death overt, with Hindley's maltreatment of him exacerbating his condition. Outside of his intensely close relationship with Catherine, he shrank from all contact with life. External reality gradually lost more and more of its import, his inner workings being his only focus. Self-centered in essence, inaccessible to others, since he was unable to direct his energies toward anything outside of himself, his only consideration was to realize what he believed to be his goal. Heathcliff, like the heroes of old—Theseus, Jason, Heracles—left Wuthering Heights to carve out his future.

The Antihero Returns

Three years pass, and Heathcliff returns from the outside world, seemingly transformed. "He had grown a tall, athletic, well-formed man. . . . His upright carriage suggested the idea of his having been in the army." Seeing him, Catherine became "breathless and wild;

too excited to show gladness: indeed, by her face, you would rather have surmised an awful calamity." Was this a premonition of what was to occur? Had she allowed that *other* side within herself to ejaculate? Was her animus cloistered so deeply within her psyche that it could no longer articulate, but merely react affectively?

Having obtained her husband's permission to invite Heathcliff to tea, she "seized Linton's reluctant fingers and crushed them into his." Mesmerized by their unification, the two archetypal beings, Catherine and Heathcliff, sat looking at each other, "too much absorbed in their mutual joy to suffer embarrassment." Words were unnecessary as sunshine poured into the room and both regressed, psychologically, to their childlike state, reliving their fantasy life inwardly. Wiser in the ways of the world since her marriage, Catherine did her utmost to control her ecstatic feelings in her husband's presence. Her play at social etiquette succeeds, for Edgar gives her permission to visit Wuthering Heights with Isabella.

The brief interlude after Heathcliff's return may be considered one of the happiest moments in Catherine's life. As an archetypal anima figure worshiped by both men, she reigned supreme in her entourage. She had succeeded in *whipping* everyone into place. Transformed in their eyes into a kind of fascinating goddess, she became Psyche, to be idolized and endowed with all of her beauteous and crystalline characteristics. The more archetypal Catherine became, however, the more alienated she grew from reality. As an inhuman or superhuman presence, she took it upon herself to regulate the lives of others, thereby cutting herself off increasingly from her human condition. No longer an earth person, she failed progressively to relate to herself and the everyday world. Finally, any commerce with anything that did not pertain to her love figure became too great for Catherine to handle. She who lived in supernal spheres experienced the *ekstasis* of the goddesses of old, before whom their votaries would bend and sway to their wishes. Destiny, however, has a way of punishing inflated beings—thus bringing them back to earth.[7]

Catherine's delicate balance prevails until Isabella falls in love with Heathcliff. It might be said that Isabella is, psychologically, the bearer of Catherine's shadow—her banal, uninteresting, mundane side that had never been given a chance to live. Angered by the very thought of a usurper altering the status quo she had so painstakingly brought about, Catherine warns Isabella: Heathcliff

would crush her, she says, "like a sparrow's egg."[8] Her attempts
to punish her sister-in-law for her insolence, for daring to attempt
to detach one of her votaries from her power, goes awry. By telling Heathcliff of Isabella's secret plans, she gives him a weapon to
avenge himself against Hindley, who had treated him ignomini-
ously; and against Edgar, whom he also despised for having taken
his Catherine from him. Although Heathcliff denies ever wanting
to hurt his beloved Catherine, unconsciously he aims his arrows
at her, for it is she who caused his wound to bleed so profusely as
to never allow healing.

Heathcliff's persona was handsome and his ways had taken on
veneer during the three years away from Wuthering Heights, but
his inner being had not altered. He marries Isabella, thus for the
first time countermanding Catherine's orders. He has, then, gath-
ered the strength to force her openly and without reserve to confront her actions. Never before had she understood or even
realized the extent of the pain she had caused Heathcliff. Obsessed with her own needs, self-indulgent in every manner and
form, she is removed from her pedestal by Heathcliff when he
tells her that her cruelty toward him was virtually unpardonable.

Traumatized by Heathcliff's words, Catherine again is faced
with incipient illness and her husband fears for her health. Moreover, he is jealous of the outsider's visit to his home. He informs
Heathcliff that his "presence is a moral poison that would contaminate the most virtuous." So powerful have the contents of
Catherine's subliminal realm become that she suffers an eclipse of
consciousness and is divested of her persona. She identifies now
with Heathcliff (her animus) against her husband, hoping that he
will flog Edgar for his ingratitude and his absurdity. Blows and
insults are forthcoming after which Heathcliff departs.

Just as Heathcliff had withdrawn to the stables and the moors
after Catherine's early rejection of him, so now, in a parallel action, she retires to her room and sees no one for three days. When
Nelly finally enters, Catherine asks her to tell Edgar, who has
spent the days reading in the library, that she is "in danger of
being seriously ill." And she adds, "I wish it may prove true."

Catherine's features have already altered as fever and hallucinations take over: she sees herself walking to her favorite spot on
the moors with Heathcliff, under Peniston Crag. In a paroxysm of
despair, regressing to her little-girl world, she yearns for her old
room at Wuthering Heights. To be in any other place is to be an

"exile and outcast" from what had been her joy and happiness. She longs to be "a girl again, half savage and hardy, and free; and laughing at injuries, not maddening under them." Unaware of her tumult and her fever, she asks Nelly to open the window so that she may fill her lungs with the aroma of the heather on the hill. Nelly refusing, Catherine walks unsteadily toward the window and opens it herself. The frosty air enfolds her as she looks out at her old room at Wuthering Heights; then, as if speaking to Heathcliff and pointing to the graveyard: "I'll not lie there by myself: they may bury me twelve feet deep, and throw the church down over me, but I won't rest till you are with me. I never will." When Edgar enters and takes her in his arms, she informs him in her delirium that he possesses her body, but "my soul will be on that hill-top before you lay hands on me again."

Diagnosed as brain fever, Catherine's illnesses were manifestations of severe psychological stress. She was unable to integrate her archetypal goddess or superhuman side with her human or natural aspect. Her choice of Edward as a husband met her demand as goddess figure, her need to shine, to climb the social ladder, but she was being untrue to her animus. Nor did she understand rationally the meaning or the impact of such a divestiture on her psyche; yet, intuitively, she knew that she was hurting herself, for she told Nelly that she would live to regret her decision. With Heathcliff's departure, she became imprisoned in her personal world and sensed unconsciously the extent of her loss each time she looked out her window to Wuthering Heights and the moors. Happiness had existed only during her free, thoughtless, and elemental childhood.

Consciousness did return to Catherine, along with a semblance of health. Edgar's solicitude throughout her illness was noteworthy: "No mother could have nursed an only child more devotedly than Edgar tended her," Nelly stated. Catherine, however, had again changed, invaded by some "unearthly beauty." Detached, she had separated herself from life.

Heathcliff eloped with Isabella, remaining away for two months. Upon the couple's return to Wuthering Heights, Isabella endured continuous martyrdom at the hands of Heathcliff: his great pleasure, he informs Nelly, is the delight he experiences in torturing his wife. "I have no pity! The more the worms writhe, the more I yearn to crush out their entrails! It is a moral teething; and I grind with greater energy, in proportion to the increase of pain."

The "moral teething" to which Heathcliff refers implies the usefulness of torture: psychologically, it enables a person to do away with his or her milk teeth, that is, infantile innocence and irresponsible behavior, that primitive identification with world parents prior to ego development and the formation of one's individuality. To accept suffering is part of the human condition.

Isabella, realizing the tragic mistake she had made by marrying Heathcliff, escapes to the south of England with her son, Hareton. Upon her death eight years later, Hareton returns to Wuthering Heights, despite Edgar's wish to bring him up in the Linton tradition.

Heathcliff did not heed Nelly's warnings: whenever he visited Catherine, her extreme nervousness and deteriorating health, including bouts of amnesia, would worsen. He is, nevertheless, determined to see her just once again. It is at this point that readers are made privy to one of the most passionate love scenes in English literature—and the most sexless.

The minute Heathcliff enters Catherine's room, he understands that there is no hope for her recovery, just as he cannot be restored to psychological health without her. In each other's arms, the two archetypal figures are like disembodied spirits. She, in utter agitation, moans her lamentations under the pain of her searing guilt, of which she is now aware: "I only wish us never to be parted: and should a word of mine distress you hereafter, think I feel the same distress underground, and for my own sake, forgive me!"

Although begging his forgiveness, she no longer has the strength to explore and understand the noxious aftermath of the cutting pain she has provoked. To escape into death, symbolizing another form of regression, would relieve her unbearable pain while allowing her to divest herself of the imprisonment of her body.

I'm tired of being enclosed here. I'm wearying to escape into that glorious world, and to be always there: not seeing it dimly through tears, and yearning for it through the walls of an aching heart; but really with it, and in it . . . in full strength: you are sorry for me—very soon that will be altered. I shall be sorry for *you*. I shall be incomparably beyond and above you all. I *wonder* he won't be near me!

Moments later she and Heathcliff are "locked in an embrace" after which he accuses her of having betrayed her own heart: "I have not broken your heart—*you* have broken it; and in breaking it, you have broken mine."

Again, she asks him to forgive her for her transgressions. "It is hard to forgive, and to look at those eyes, and feel those wasted hands. . . . Kiss me again; and don't let me see your eyes! I forgive what you have done to me. I love *my* murderer—but *yours!* How can I?"

At Edgar's approach, Heathcliff attempts to extricate himself from her grasp, Catherine is already at the threshold between two worlds—the living and the dead, the real and the unreal. The barriers protecting her feeble ego have weakened and the collective forces within her psyche have flowed forth, allowing her to fall under the spell of nonpersonal powers.

Catherine's child Cathy is born on that very night; two hours later, she dies in perfect peace, without ever having recovered sufficient consciousness to recognize either Heathcliff or Edgar. After Catherine's demise, Heathcliff's passion became ungovernable.

Catherine Earnshaw, may you not rest as long as I am living. You said I killed you—haunt me, then! The murdered *do* haunt their murderers, I believe. I know that ghosts *have* wandered on earth. Be with me always—take any form—drive me mad! Only *do* not leave me in this abyss, where I cannot find you! Oh, God! it is unutterable! I *cannot* live without my life! I *cannot* live without my soul!

Living in a world of disembodied souls, as a *ghost*, Heathcliff found that reality had no longer any meaning for him. Catherine alone lived as a powerful force within him, haunting his every move and moment. Increasingly autistic and unreachable, Heathcliff was still bent upon destroying those and their offspring who had wronged him. He had used sadistic acts and cruelties of all types as mechanisms to diffuse his hatred at the injustices he had to endure throughout his life. To destroy those upon whom one projects such venom, is, psychologically, an attempt to do violence to oneself.

Hindley was his first victim: his drinking, dissolute, and half-demented behavior, as well as his gambling at cards, enabled Heathcliff to gain possession of Wuthering Heights and the farm. Hindley's son, Hareton, to whom Heathcliff denied all education and relegated to the stable as plowboy, was completely dependent upon the new master. Because Hareton—unlike his father—

"writhing like a worm"—was stalwart, courageous, and open, Heathcliff took no pleasure in torturing him. In fact, he sees him as "gold put to the use of paving stones" and, strangely enough, wins the lad's affection. Isabella's son, Linton, claimed by Heathcliff after his mother's demise, was frail, delicate, and self-centered. Detested by Heathcliff for his timorous nature and spoiled manner, he is described by him as "tin polished to ape silver." Cathy, brought up by her father Edgar, with great care and tenderness, turns out to be far more human and psychologically healthier than her mother. Heathcliff intends to keep Linton alive until such time as he marries Cathy, thereby uniting the Lintons' fortune with his own. Although aware of her future husband's worthless nature, Cathy accepts her fate, rising to the occasion by striking back at Heathcliff's vulnerability.

Linton is all I have to love in the world, and though you have done what you could to make him hateful to me, and me to him, you *cannot* make us hate each other. And I defy you to hurt him when I am by, and I defy you to frighten me!

I know he has a bad nature . . . he's your son. But I'm glad I've a better, to forgive it; and I know he loves me, and for that reason I love him. Mr. Heathcliff, *you* have *nobody* to love you; and, however miserable you make us, we shall still have the revenge of thinking that your cruelty arises from your greater misery. You *are* miserable, are you not? Lonely, like the devil, and envious like him? *Nobody* loves you—*nobody* will cry for you when you die. I wouldn't be you!

Although Cathy's sorrow is great when her father dies, unlike her mother she is strong and compassionate toward others. She marries Linton and when he becomes mortally sick, it is she, the seventeen-year-old, who struggles alone in the room with death, since Heathcliff refuses to call the doctor. In time, although Cathy was at first repulsed by Hareton's boorishness and lack of culture, mocking him as had her mother when comparing Heathcliff with Edgar, she senses, then sees the *gold* within him. Refusing the easy way out—she could have married the rich Lockwood who is intrigued by her beauty, thereby escaping her tormentor, she accepts her suffering, and as Hareton had, so will not writhe like a worm. She teaches her husband to read, the first step in carving out a new life for themselves. Aware of the cruelty she had meted out to Hareton, she comes to realize what her mother had never understood, that intellectual accomplishments and social graces may be acquired, but not character.

Cathy has still more to learn about life in general, and her relationship with Hareton in particular. When she attempts to enlighten him concerning Heathcliff's bestial behavior, Hareton defends him "by ties stronger than reason could break—chains forged by habit that it would be cruel to attempt to loosen."[9] Cathy now understands that she must not speak against their common oppressor, that she must accept Hareton's love for Heathcliff no matter how distasteful it might appear to her. Only then would she be accepting Hareton *whole* and be free to love him as her husband.

As Cathy's consciousness expands, so Heathcliff's desire to hurt her and those in his household decreases. Without the energy invested in vengeance and hatred, he experiences more powerfully the presence of his beloved Catherine in his every thought and feeling. His "entire world is a dreadful collection of memoranda that she [Catherine] did exist and that I have lost her." He notes a change in himself: "I take so little interest in my daily life that I hardly remember to eat and drink." More and more passive, "I have to remind myself to breathe—almost remind my heart to beat!" Daily he eats less and less, starving himself, as Catherine had, into disembodiment. His single wish, to be reunited with his beloved, must have so preoccupied him that he forgot to breathe. One morning Nelly finds him dead in the bed he and Catherine had shared when they were children, the bed in which Lockwood had had his dream.

I hasped the window; I combed his black long hair from his forehead; I tried to close his eyes: to extinguish, if possible, that frightful, life-like gaze of exultation before any one else beheld it. They would not shut: they seemed to sneer at my attempts: and his parted lips and sharp white teeth sneered too!

Catherine had succeeded in drawing him to her, to the grave she would now share with him. The archetypal pair did not survive; Cathy and Hareton, the human couple, did live on in a happiness based on commitment, understanding, and compassion for one another—and humanity in general.

Heathcliff's work of uniting the two polarities of a soul, two conscious principles, in Hareton and Cathy, had been accomplished. The young couple were married on New Year's Day, the fortune of the Earnshaws and Lintons passing down to them; while their immortal counterparts continued to live their love in the eternality of the archetype that has and will continue to fascinate humankind the world over.

So, too, would Emily live on, not as poet, but as the creator of her myth, as embodied in Catherine and Heathcliff, in *Wuthering Heights*, the dramatization of an archetypal unfolding emanating from the very depths of her being.

5

Charlotte Brontë: "If You Knew My Thoughts...."

Unloved I love, unwept I weep,
Grief I restrain, hope I repress;
Vain is this anguish, fixed and deep,
Vainer desires or means of bliss....

Come Reason—Science—Learning—Thought—
To you my heart I dedicate;
I have a faithful subject brought:
Faithful because most desolate....

It [spirit] wakes but to be crushed again:
Faint I will not, nor yield to sorrow;
Conflict and force will quell the brain;
Doubt not I shall be strong tomorrow.[1]

Conflict between Charlotte's tempestuous passions that she, through religious beliefs, sought to temper, and her unending desire to write is evident in her work as far back as her juvenilia. Her early works reveal innumerable moral pressures. Indeed, the more she indulged her fantasy world, the greater was her sense of guilt. How could she reconcile the evil acts of her protagonists—their jealousies, deceits, bloodcurdling killings, and infidelities—to her Christian values? By emphasizing the "infernal" nature of her characters, she felt a deep sense of betrayal to her God, and sought some way of combining her creativity with the need to be true to herself and Divinity. Was she a victim of the Anti-Christ? The kind of writing in which she was indulging was both *evil* and *unfeminine*, but she nevertheless felt compelled to turn out her torrid and cruel romances à la Scott and Byron.

Since Charlotte's juvenilia stirred guilt and anxiety in her, one wonders why she did not put a halt to the flow of her pen? Charlotte's acute spiritual distress with regard to her thematics is evident in many of her letters to her friend and former school-mate, Ellen Nussey.

Don't deceive yourself by imagining that I have a bit of real goodness about me. My darling if I were like you I should have my face Zionward though prejudice and error might occasionally fling a mist over the glorious vision before me for with all your single-hearted sincerity you have your faults, but I am *not like you*. If you knew my thoughts; the dreams that absorb me; and the fiery imagination that at times eats me up and makes me feel Society as it is, wretchedly insipid, you would pity and I dare say despise me. But Ellen I know the treasures of the Bible I love and adore them I can *see* the Well of Life in all its clearness and brightness; but when I stoop down to drink of the pure waters they fly from my lips as if I were Tantalus.[2]

The Poems: "Unloved I Love, Unwept I Weep"

The poems interspersed in Charlotte's juvenilia (1829–39) reveal not only the richness of her fantasy world and the range of her emotions, but the germs of her future novels as well. So powerful was her imagination, so repressed her instincts and sexual desires, that her poetry—a bridge between her outer and inner worlds—took on the luster of the life she longed for but could not live.

That Charlotte named the wooden soldier Branwell had offered her "Duke of Wellington" may shed light on the thematics and conflictual elements implicit in her poetry. The Iron Duke, as he was called, was an outstanding figure: chief in command following the death of Sir John Moore (1761–1809) in the Peninsular War (1809), England's representative at the Congress of Vienna (1814–15), defeater of Napoléon at Waterloo (1815), and prime minister of Britain (1828–30). That such a personality was Charlotte's idol reveals her own ambitious nature.

The wealth of Charlotte's poems revolving around romances and cataclysmic confrontations in which her hero and his two sons (Arthur, Lord Douro, and Charles Wellesley) were involved, intimates the complexity of the repressed powers she harbored within her. Never better were these revealed than in "Mementos," a multilayered treasure trove of ideas and feelings. Slowly, but with point and dexterity, Charlotte yields her secrets in confessional tones. Images and rhythms alter in pace as excitement grows, as characters destroy or build, spreading tyranny, tragedy, turmoil, or the serenity of beauteous joy, as in "The Wife's Will."

A change in Charlotte's poetry and prose occurred after her return from Roe Head. No longer was the Duke of Wellington dominating the limelight; his sons, Arthur Wellesley and Lord Douro were now dominant. No longer were political power and incipient wars and conquests thematically important. Love and knightly escapades, separations and rescues, wrought with elegance and a sense of rectitude, took precedence—as in "Frances."

> Who can for ever crush the heart,
>   Restrain its throbbing, curb its life?
> Dissemble truth with ceaseless art,
>   With outward calm mask inward strife?

Instead of featuring the prim, pure, and passively virginal heroines opted for at the outset of her Angrian adventures, she chose illicit relationships, fiery passions, and a panoply of cloak-and-dagger escapades, replete with infidelities, jealousies, and outbreaks of cataclysmic turbulence.

By 1839 Charlotte, perhaps to break away from Branwell and fend for herself as a writer or perhaps because her respect for her brother deteriorated after his trip to London and his failure to apply to the Royal Academy of Arts, ended her participation in the Angrian Cycle. In "Parting" she tells us:

> There's no use in weeping,
> Though we are condemned to part;
> There's such a thing as keeping
> A remembrance in one's heart. (1838)

Perhaps the intrigues and passionate encounters of the many venal creatures of her fantasy had finally come into such conflict with her highly moral and religious credo that she could no longer bear to pursue such "ignominious" ways? Or was it a question of mastery of style? Her spontaneous and uncrafted writing evident in her Glass Town and Angrian chronicles may no longer have satisfied her aesthetic inclinations? It might also be suggested that she had outgrown the high-pressured plots and counterplots, the facile passions and frenzied encounters of the paper-thin destinies she had until now impressed upon paper.

More substance, greater artistry, and authenticity of character
may now have been her goal.

Charlotte's stay at the Pensionnat Héger (1842–44) was a turning point in her life. So desperate had been her passion for her
mentor, Mr. Constantine Héger, that her dreams suffered invasion
by sexual and spiritual images, creating such havoc within her that
she resigned her post and left for Haworth. Once at home, her
brooding despair over her unrequited passion turned productive.
For the first time in her life she had experienced—viscerally as
well as spiritually—*real* feelings for a man. No longer would she
be wedged into depicting sequences of flighty and fanciful plots.
Henceforth she would deal with her own storehouse of memories,
the very meat and core of life. After the publication of *Poems by
Currer, Ellis, and Acton Bell* (1846), she began work on a novel,
The Professor. Despite the six rejections she received from publishers, eroding her pride, she refused to accept failure passively.
A fighter and survivor, she began *Jane Eyre,* which was accepted
by Smith, Elder and Company and won immediate acclaim. Publication of *The Professor,* however, was posthumous (1857).

THE NOVELS

The Professor: Antagonisms Resolved

Written with the grace and charm of many a Victorian novel, *The
Professor* also possesses a psychologically fascinating quality of
its own. Unlike *Wuthering Heights,* neither the happenings nor
the characters emanate from the author's archetypal depths; they
are not, therefore, mythical in stature. More like *Agnes Grey, The
Professor* is a structured and rationally conceived work, an attempt on the author's part to perfect and restrain the formerly
effulgent style of her juvenilia.

The writing of *The Professor* may have served as a means to
clarify Charlotte's thoughts concerning the art of the novelist. Every move and thought of the protagonists, within a set frame-
work and ambiance, gives the impression of having been churned
and rechurned, sifted, fleshed out, and evaluated in the author's
logical mind and within the preconceived plot line. Although
spontaneous events do occur at strategic moments in the novel,
they are designed to illuminate the characters' own weaknesses

and foibles, thus giving them another chance to pursue the best and most righteous of courses. As in *Agnes Grey*, integrity and forthrightness are uppermost in the outlook of hero and heroine. Nevertheless, the power of passion pulsates, albeit in diminished and most always controlled sequences. Although hatred, jealousy, anger, and the purest and most naive of notions are interwoven in the very fabric of *The Professor*, these emotions are used as literary strategies designed to heighten or slacken suspense. So thought out is *The Professor* that the feelings motivating the protagonists' actions give the impression of having been built into the very lining of their personalities, thus divesting them of any authenticity. Still, the touches of morbidity and the sequences focusing on the male protagonist's sexual awakening are sufficiently complex to give the reader pause.

Like Marcel Proust who, in *Remembrance of Things Past*, transformed many a male into a female character and vice versa, thus enabling him to conceal certain anomalies, so Charlotte, unwilling to lay bare tendencies embedded within her own psyche that could possibly be offensive to Victorian readers, altered the sexual identities of her characters. She seemed to feel greater ease using a male protagonist as spokesman to disclose her feelings and thoughts than a female.

Most arresting in *The Professor* is the in-depth psychological study of hatred existing between two brothers, Edward and William Crimsworth. So understanding is the author of the problems involved, so sensitive is she to the nuances of their needs and motivations that one is inclined to consider them somewhat autobiographical in nature. Is the seething antagonism implicit in *The Professor* a manifestation of her relationship with Emily and Anne? Or are the two brothers to be viewed as doubles—concretizations of polarities buried within her own psyche? The theme of the double is not without precedent, as, for example, Poe's "William Wilson," Dostoyevsky's *The Double*, and Gogol's *Diary of a Madman*.

Brother Hatred: An Operative Shadow

The first part of *The Professor*, which takes place in England, focuses on the bitter enmity existing between Edward and William Crimsworth. Such hostility, viewed psychologically, occurs when a shadow projection is operative.

The shadow is that part of the unconscious personality containing inferior characteristics that the individual is unwilling or as yet unable to recognize as his own and, therefore, projects onto another or others. William, the narrator, is oblivious to the fact that the "evils" he condemns in his brother are the very ones he detests and seeks to annihilate in himself. Condemning Edward freely and without any self-examination, William maintains his own sense of integrity and righteousness on the surface at least. More serious is the fact that the longer he attributes to his brother characteristics he cannot or is unwilling to accept as his own—allowing hatred, rage, and antagonism to be meted out freely to Edward—there can be no increase in self-knowledge on his part.

What is the basis of the hatred existing between the two brothers? Both are orphans. Their father, having failed as a mill owner, died six months before William's birth; the mother succumbed in childbirth. Having been repudiated by their wealthy and aristocratic maternal family, who had never forgiven Mrs. Crimsworth for having married beneath her station, the brothers were brought up with the minimum of charity by their father's uncles. Only by dint of threats from other members of the family does William receive support and go to Eton. Unwilling to enter the church upon his graduation, the twenty-year-old William opts for a business career. To this end, he seeks out his thirty-year-old brother, Edward, who through hard work, ingenuity, and a good marriage, has become a successful mill owner at Bigben Close in the North of England. Jealous of William's Etonian education, Edward harbors no warmth for his brother, and offers him a relatively low job—a second clerkship—for someone so well educated.

Although both brothers had been orphaned, Edward was ten when his parents died, and had suffered most grievously from their loss, while William had never really known them. On the other hand, Edward had benefited from his mother's love, whereas William, deprived of all maternal feeling, had been divested of all sense of belonging, warmth, and well-being. Did Edward unconsciously consider William a murderer, blaming him for his mother's demise, since she died in childbirth?

Edward's overtly destructive responses to William may be viewed as projections of negative characteristics lodged deeply within William and not necessarily contents belonging to the wealthy mill owner. It may be suggested that both Edward and William are split-offs of *one* person—the shadow side of each juxtaposed to the positive aspects of the other. Since Edward is the more emotional of the two, and affects usually emerge when adaptation is weakest, his uncontrollable behavioral patterns disclose an inability to cope with his sense of inferiority.[3]

The day after his first visit to Crimsworth Hall, Edward's "Good Morning" to William was abrupt, after which he "snatched" a newspaper from the table and began reading it "with the air of a master who seizes a pretext to escape the bore of conversing with an underling." There was no dialogue between the two. William repressed his hurt. As he was cogitating about how best he could endure his brother's insults while maintaining, at least on the outside, a courteous stance, he happened to see Edward's reflection in the mirror. But was it actually Edward's countenance that he had viewed? Or was he in fact looking upon those secret and unacceptable qualities within his own self that he had projected onto his brother? But then, William rationalized, the qualities in which his brother excelled were merely physical or "animal." As an intellectual, the younger brother considered himself superior to the business man, and has decided to "force" his mind to learn to cope with the situation at hand. As a thinking person, he was determined to force his will to dominate any emotional encounter and any unconscious pulsations that might spin off from their meeting. To assess his brother's personality might yield positive results; it would not only give William the key to his future comportment, but would help him extricate himself from an unpleasant present situation. For example, he understood that he could expect no "lion-like generosity" from his brother; nor did Edward's stern and forbidding manner augur well for the birth of any kind of relationship between the two. The consideration of both brothers as dual aspects of a *single* personality, foretells incompatibility within that one individual.

Because "Caution, Tact, Observation" determined William's behavioral patterns, his life became increasingly solitary. His practice of self-analysis, however, encouraged him to *question* his motives, needs, and desires, and to listen to his inner voice for "a clear notion" of what he was, what he wanted, and how much unhappiness he would be able to endure. He came to understand finally that were he to remain for any length of time in his brother's employ, he would not only not derive any emotional compensation from his work, but would, on the contrary, stagnate and even regress. Neither warmth nor understanding nor even a texture of friendship could be expected. The psychological condition of stasis he was suffering is reflected in the iciness of his rented room, in which the maid always forgot to light an evening fire. Without fire, an agent of transformation, no feelings or love could be born. Only rigidity.

Two factors intervened encouraging William to change his course. The first was William's chance meeting with Mr. Hunsden, a manufacturer and mill owner who saw how diligent a worker he was and how ill-treated he had been by his brother. In Hunsden's rooms, the "bright grate was filled with a genuine—shire fire, red, clear, and generous." It was Hunsden, a fire principle, who advised William to strike out on his own. What career would be to his liking? was the question. Teaching was the answer. Whereupon, Mr. Hunsden wrote a letter of introduction to a well-placed man in Brussels, who might be in a position to offer William a post as a teacher. The second event precipitating William's departure was his brutal and unjust dismissal by Edward whose wrath had been aroused by the rumor that William had spoken ill of him.

Only one object had arrested William's attention during the three months he spent working for his brother: the portrait of his mother hanging at Crimsworth Hall. So important had it become for him that it symbolically pointed to the next step in his maturing process: the seeking out the *mother* image, the carrier and embodiment of the feminine principle—known as anima in the male.

Anima as Feminine Principle

The personification of the feminine principle, the *anima,* as previously defined, is "an autonomous psychic content in the male personality"; an inner woman, or the "psychic representation of the contrasexual elements in man."[4] When a man's anima is projected onto a living woman, it leads him to fall in love. If he is involved with a willful, devouring, and demonic type, and if his projection is unconscious, his ego may be submerged by the power she has over him and reduce him to a state of paralysis or childlike obedience to her. If, on the other hand, he is conscious of his anima, and his ego is sufficiently developed, she may lead him to know a meaningful and profound relationship.

A Negative Anima

Upon his arrival in Brussels, and thanks to Hunsden's intervention, William obtains a post as English and Latin teacher in a boy's school directed and owned by a M. Pelet. Although surprised by the mediocre intellectual level of the students, William enjoys his new post and earns respect and confidence. He pleasures in Mr. Pelet's company and is able to relate to this "clever and witty" Frenchman.

One of the windows of William's room overlooked the garden of the girl's school opposite, and decency had dictated that it should be boarded to prevent a prying eye from peering into feminine mysteries. Utterly naïve in matters of sex or anything remotely identified with womankind, William was excited about the very thought of such an interdict. When alone, he tried to find some chink or hole in the boarded-up window that might allow him to "peep at the consecrated ground." Although his efforts were to no avail, the thought of the *"allée defendue"* aroused sexual awareness in him. How much he would have enjoyed spying on these forbidden delights is conveyed metaphorically—as a beautiful garden with flowers and trees, somewhat reminiscent of a Garden of Eden.

So one-sided was William's upbringing, so identified was he with the spirit rather than with anything relating to the human sphere, that when Mr. Pelet's mother invites him to *goûter,* he is convinced that she seeks to make love to him! Mrs. Pelet's invitation is, however, business-oriented, and leads to the contrived offer to William of a position as English teacher at the "Pensionnat des demoiselles" adjacent to Mr. Pelet's academy. "I shall now at last see the mysterious garden, I shall gaze both on the angels and their Eden," William thinks.

Zoraide Reuter, director of the girls' pensionnat, was an anima figure: a seductress capable of leading William step-by-step into the world of feminine mysteries. Bewitching by her demeanor from the very outset, she, like the goddesses of antiquity, aroused in William hitherto unknown sensations of love.

In reality, Zoraide was an illusion-creating anima figure who sought, perhaps unconsciously at first, then with open determination, to envelop, embrace, and devour her prey. A negative feminine principle, she represented danger to the naïve, deception to the morally sound, and suffering to the gullible. It was only a matter of time before William would be caught in her web, and left there to strangle helplessly.

Unaware of her power over him, however, William blithely became enticed by Zoraide's bewitching feminine charm. Each time he returned from the girl's school, happiness rather than his usual somberness was imprinted on his features and his confidence and competence as a teacher also improved.

Mr. Pelet, aware of William's naïveté in terms of the opposite sex, was quick to point out to him that "any woman, sinking her shaft deep enough, will at last reach a fathomless spring of sensibility in thy breast." Believing that God's light was shining upon him and Zoraide, William was all the more unprepared for the cruel deception that was forthcoming: leaning out of his window one evening to look down on the very spot that had witnessed the first and most delectable discussion with his ladylove, he overheard a conversation between her and Mr. Pelet, which revealed that they were secretly engaged and had encouraged his infatuation simply for amusement. So deeply shocked is William that he swears to maintain henceforth a stone-cold countenance toward Zoraide.

Perplexed, because she cannot account for the sudden change in William's behavior, Zoraide becomes attracted to his invulnerability and impassibility. Using her wiles, she does her best to soften his hostility; and to impress him with her altruism, she tells of her kindness toward a poor young English-Swiss seamstress in the school's employ, Frances Evans Henri.

A Positive Anima

If Zoraide may be considered a negative anima type, interested only in gratifying her own desires and calculating how best to ensnare and then devour her prey, Frances Evans Henri was her antithesis. Natural, innocent, methodical, and candid, she also possessed a certain winsomeness. Although spiritually oriented, she was firmly rooted to this earth, but had no illusions about life or people. She conformed to expectations both as an employee in the school and in the city, but being ambitious, she sought to improve her command of the English language and eventually gain access to better employment.

As anima, she embodied William's suprapersonal values or ideal. Like the *femme inspiratrice,* she would unconsciously play an indispensable role in his world, knowing instinctively how to focus on her own goals, and at the same time help William to function at his best under dismal circumstances. As anima, her qualities reflected his own rich unconscious feminine side.

Frances would not only play the role of the beloved, but also that of a nourishing and kindly mother figure. She would fill the void in William's heart, which had been created when he looked so longingly at the portrait of his mother hanging in Edward's home. Coincidentally, it was this very painting that Mr. Hunsden, on a visit to Brussels, had brought to William, telling him that he had bought it at an auction sale following Edward's bankruptcy.

William becomes increasingly impressed by Frances's intelligence and her beautiful character traits. Unspoiled, demure, even shy at times, she is endowed with perseverance, a sense of duty, and an extraordinary ability to contend with life's difficulties. Her integrity is antipodal to the moral unsoundness of Zoraide who, now jealous of Frances, summarily dismisses her. The "perfidious" vamp, dominated by a "vice-polluted soul," resorts to the lie, telling William that the little seamstress employed by the school has resigned her post and left no forwarding address.

Fruitlessly, William makes inquiry everywhere hoping to discover Frances's whereabouts. Finally resigning his teaching post, he sets out in search of her in the city, visiting even the Protestant cemetery in Brussels. It is there that he finds her, beside the grave of her last living relative, her recently departed aunt. Although William realizes he is in love with Frances, he cannot propose to her until he finds a new situation. Disheartening weeks follow. Finally, thanks to the father of one of his former students whom he had saved from drowning, he obtains a fine teaching position, proposes to Frances, and is accepted.

Accustomed to supporting herself in life, Frances—a good feminist—is determined to keep on working as a lacemaker and mender, even after marriage, despite William's wish that she remain a homebody. Her determined refusal is quiet but steadfast. No human power could bend her will. "Think of my marrying you to be kept by you, Monsieur! I could not do it—and how dull my days would be!" By dint of the couple's hard work, in ten years time they amassed sufficient capital to enable them and their son, Victor, to retire to England, Frances's "Promised Land."

Charlotte's expository discourse in *The Professor* concludes without being judgmental. She succeeded in cutting open the bruised soul of her protagonist—a manifestation of her own—but she did not know how to express the workings of the masculine psyche. William's needs and ideations seem contrived, awkward,

and conveyed in stilted language, and, as the reviewer for the
North British Review wrote:

It is quite obvious to any reader who attends to the sketch of the character of the Professor, that the Professor is a woman in disguise, . . . for
she is quite properly stripped of her male costume . . . There is a shyness,
a sulky tenderness, and a disposition to coquet manifest in the Professor's
relations with his friend . . . which betrays to us at once that the picture
is drawn from a lady's experience of her friendship with the other sex.[5]

Jane Eyre: Signs, Symbols, and the Preternatural Experience

Jane Eyre (1847) is a feminist novel par excellence. Readers are
spared no detail as they follow the plight of a penniless orphan,
ill-treated by the family sheltering her, then suffering further dep-
rivations and humiliations as a pupil in a school for the poor. Affliction and grief, however, are the means through which Jane learns
not only to cope with some of life's problems, but also to carve out
a destiny for herself, which includes a passionate love experience.

The Red Room

The image of the *Red Room,* used symbolically by Charlotte at
the outset of the novel, points up the psychologically injurious
nature of Jane's early years, from infancy to the age of ten, spent
in the home of her aunt, Mrs. Reed, who transfers her own frustrations—blending anger and venom—on the defenseless Jane.
The most traumatic of the child's protracted punishments was
confinement in the "red room," which she believed to be haunted.
No warmth, understanding, or tenderness is received by Jane,
who is also taunted and brutalized by Mrs. Reed's three spoiled
children—particularly her son, John. Thrust on her own resources, the lonely waif lives the life of an exile. Here is an inward journey, perilous, tremulous, and painful.

That the red-room episode should have occurred at Gateshead,
the name of Mrs. Reed's estate, is significant. Onomastically,
Gateshead reinforces Jane's psychological condition of alienation
and sense of imprisonment in a hopeless situation: a *gate* serves
as a barrier preventing any free-flowing communication between
the protagonist and the outside world; *head* implies Jane's psychological need to develop the thinking side of her personality

while keeping her feeling world in check. She had to function analytically, through her *head* or *mind,* and keep her heart and emotions tightly sealed behing the *gate.*

Her restrictive ambiance not only activated bouts of despair in Jane, but also fired the volatile instinctual realm within her psyche. The hermetic sealing of one part of a person encourages an eventful flaring up of incarcerated forces. So powerful may these excoriating energetic charges become that they can no longer be contained, and ignite in sequences of uncontrollable episodes, with understandably devastating results.

To seek peace of mind, Jane would frequently sit in the window seat in the small breakfast room, drawing the *scarlet* drapery around her and thus shutting herself off from the Reed family. A sequence of metonymies—a cold winter scene with its "leafless shrubbery," its "raw twilight," its "storm-beat shrub," its "ceaseless rain sweeping away wildly before a long and lamentable blast"—reveals her condition of psychological deprivation. Within the relatively protected area, encircled symbolically by a fiery curtain, she was able not only to read her favorite books, but to gaze through the window towards freedom. After the fourteen-year-old John reprimands Jane, "a dependent" without money, for reading one of *his* books, he snatches it and flings it at Jane, who, in her attempt to avoid it, falls and strikes her head against the door. Cut and bleeding, she flashes out verbally: "Wicked and cruel boy!... murderer." John informs his mother of the incident and Jane is immediately locked up in the red room.

The "room," an enclosed area, is the locus of Jane's agon or struggle. Psychologically, her imprisonment in the red chamber may be viewed as a testing ground—an initiation—thus giving it ritualistic connotations. Functioning as a secret space, it is within this inner area that the heroine will begin to deal with her fears and learn to confront the vagaries of the life experience. Such a trial, undergone by so many heroines and heroes of past times, if successful, endows an initiate with the strength necessary to step into the next stage of development.

The color red, so horror provoking a hue for Jane, has ritualistic significance when identified with fire, warmth, and blood. Empirically speaking, red/blood is a life-giving and life-sustaining force. Because of Jane's highly religious orientation, red may be associated with the blood sacrifice of Christ in Holy Communion, which allows the initiate to bathe in transpersonal spheres. Red also stands for those earth-factors Jane represses: raw instinct, uncontrolled inner urges, and sexual passion.

To be incarcerated in the red room triggers an outpouring of Jane's demons of the night. Since her uncle, Mr. Reed, her mother's brother, had died in the room, she is convinced that his ghost will come to life and haunt her. It was he who had asked Mrs. Reed to bring Jane up as one of her own; because she had not done so, his soul was not at peace. Unable to fight the demons hidden in the walls, ceilings, floorboards, and draperies of the red room, the lonely and rejected child, brought up on the ghost stories of the Gothic novels of the time, understandably was terrified by imprisonment in a pitch-black room furnished with dark mahogany furniture and a predominantly red decor.

Like the initiates of the Eleusinian mysteries in Greece who had to descend into a darkened room deep within Mother Earth, so Jane faced her ordeal in Mrs. Reed's eerie and shadowy red room, which assumed fearsome religious connotations. Around the bed, "which stood out like a tabernacle in the centre" of the room, hung deep red damask curtains; blinds drawn over the windows were covered by red draperies, thus shutting out the little light that might seep into this inner sanctum.

The use of the word *tabernacle,* referring to the bed in which Jane's uncle had died, may be associated with the chalice that holds the consecrated elements of the Eucharist, or the ornamental ciborium over a high altar, thus adding a religious value to Jane's experience. It is within this cold and silent locked red room, removed from the living area of Gateshead Hall, that Jane will live out her exile, her spiritual blood communion with extratemporal forces, and her bodily initiation by eucharistic bread communion.

Mirrors placed here and there in the red room added to Jane's turmoil and disorientation. The large looking glass into which Jane stared from time to time during her imprisonment not only reflected the gloss of the dark panels of the wardrobe, but "repeated the vacant majesty of the bed and room." The sensation of emptiness implied an inner void within Jane's psyche, a gaping maw representing an entire unlived and perhaps awesome dimension of her life. It was this vast vacant area that, the longer Jane spent locked in the red room, become increasingly alive with bristling energy, feelings, and sensations, and with all sorts of terrifying amorphous matter and invisible phantoms.

The mirror, which duplicates appearances, cuts, reflects, and deflects patterned sequences, may also be understood in terms of its Latin root, *speculum*. Serving to encourage speculation, self-contemplation, and understanding, mirrors as containers of unconscious memories not only reflect these potent forces, but participate in them. They subject these memories, and the one who projects upon them—in this instance Jane—to transformation. As Jane peered into the looking glass, she began to recall one by one the cases of mistreatment she had received at the hands of the Reed family: reviled for her dark skin, although John also had the same coloring, punished unjustly, humiliated—all served to increase her own self-doubt. Jane resolved to become as perfect as possible, to commit no fault and to fulfill all duties expected of her, thus taking up the best arms she knew to fight her battle.

Complex and contradictory, the mirror not only serves to reproduce, contain, and absorb images, but, for superstitious people such as Jane, is endowed with the magical and supernatural function of invoking apparitions and ghosts. Used as an instrument of divination in ancient Persia, Greece, and Egypt, the mirror resurrected the souls of the dead. Perhaps Jane's uncle, too, would return, to add to her terror of nocturnal apparitions and presences. Yet, she could not help but turn "a fascinated eye towards the dimly gleaming mirror"—that object capable of evoking the return of dead men whose last wishes had been violated in order to "punish the perjured and avenge the oppressed."

The dread of ghostly presences is not unusual in high-strung, morbid, and anguished people who fear persecution by others. Materialized disembodied intelligences emanating from another world represent forces returning to haunt both the guilty and the innocent. "Fearful lest any sign of violent grief might waken a preternatural voice to comfort me," Jane was determined to hide her tears, hush her sobs, stifle her terror, and devour her fear. When moonbeams began to penetrate a slight aperture in the blind, stirring a complex of mirror images, whose prismatic reflections took on awesome quivering qualities, her heart beat faster, her head grew hot, and her ears filled with sounds of rushing wings. Compelled to run to the door and shake the lock, she screamed out her anguish—and then fainted.

To Mr. Lloyd, the apothecary called in to minister to her, Jane was able to convey her "inexpressible sadness" and her "wretchedness of mind." Her "illness" was followed by further punishment and segregation. Feelings of "ire and desperate revolt," which had been repressed for so long, were gaining momentum once again, seething and burning, until one day, unable to accept John's jeering and sneering, Jane struck him with her knuckles on the nose, releasing her affective side to such an extent that she felt unburdened of great stores of pent-up inner rage.

Now it was decided that Jane should be sent away to school. Reverend Brocklehurst, the director of the Lowood charity institution, was an intimidating presence: "a black pillar" whose grim face resembled "a carved mask," who became for her an incarnation of Evil. A composite of the Devil and the Wolf in Red Riding Hood, he was a *devourer* of little children and of sacrificial victims. It was during her interview with this formidably negative presence that Mrs. Reed described Jane as deceitful and hateful. "I dimly perceived that she was already obliterating hope from the new phase of existence which she destined me to enter."

Before leaving Gateshead Hall for Lowood School, Jane poured out her hatred for Mrs. Reed and for her "miserable cruelty," thus unburdening herself still further. The experience in the red room had been traumatic but also cathartic for Jane. The energy released by the discharge of inner tension after fainting gave her the strength to take the first step in further ejecting repressed unpleasantnesses into consciousness. Her ability to abreact these emotions expanded her awareness into her own problems, thus encouraging her to try to determine her own future behavior patterns and emotional attitudes.

The Lowood School: A Miasmic Internment

Jane left for Lowood early on a chill dark January morning. Seized by ambivalent feelings, she pleasured at the thought of leaving Gateshead Hall for unknown, remote, and mysterious regions, but was prey to uneasiness at the thought of the unforeseeable at Lowood School. Her cogitations, combined with the regular rhythms of the carriage passing through town after town during her fifty-mile trip, lulled Jane into a sleep similar to her faint, although not as violent. Again experiencing an eclipse of consciousness, she is temporarily released from her anxieties by the nutritive and restorative force of sleep.

Although Jane's hopes for the future ran high and she believed that anything would be better than her tortured existence at Mrs.

Reed's home, Lowood proved to be even more imprisoning, albeit in a different way. The teachers, with few exceptions, were sadistic in their treatment of the utterly regimented students. Floggings and vilifications were meted out at the slightest provocation. Since asceticism was the rule of the day, Jane's physical suffering increased dramatically at Lowood School. The building was kept so cold that water froze inside the rooms; food was at a premium, and the girls were forever hungry. Despite the rigorous physical and spiritual atmosphere, Jane studied with pleasure and each day struggled through her difficult and painful tasks with renewed purpose.

Reverend Brocklehurst's visit to Lowood marked a turning point in Jane's life. When "the black marble clergyman" spied the trembling Jane among the student body, he had her come forth and stand erect on a stool before all the students. Repeating Mrs. Reed's appelations of Jane, he accused her of being a "liar," a "castaway," an "alien," and warned them all to be on their guard, to shun and "exclude her" from their sports: "punish her body to save her soul." Reverend Brocklehurst then ordered Jane to stand on a stool for a half hour, *exposed* to the view of everyone around her. That Jane endured her feelings of humiliation— her martyrdom—likened her to some of the saints of old, thus transforming her into a type of heroine. Instead of becoming hysterical, she ordered her body to take a "firm stand on the stool."

The regressive image represented by Reverend Brocklehurst and most of the teaching staff, fostered a static, stifling, stultifying, and stagnant atmosphere to dominate at Lowood. Under such conditions, it is not surprising to learn that a degenerative and insalubrious climate festered. Lowood became a breeding ground for unbalanced and unacknowledged inner frustrations, for the increase of degenerate instincts and emotional deposits to pullulate in the darkened world of the unconscious.

So extreme was the retrograde dogma at Lowood that any deviation, be it the smallest of infractions, was punishable by the most brutal of methods. Driven by the notion of asceticism, repulsed—at least on the outside—by the thought of sexuality, the hallmark of evil, darkness ruled the precincts. Diseased minds gave birth to diseased bodies.

It was May, when "blue sky, placid sunshine, and soft western or southern gales" encourage the burgeoning of new life. Hidden beneath Mother Nature's exquisite opulence, however, exists her other shadowy and destructive side. Lowood, as the name indicates, had been built in the midst of a forestead and low-lying area, "the cradle of fog bred pestilence." The outbreak of typhus virtually decimated the school. Like Thebes, under the reign of Oedipus and Jocasta, and the Fisher King's mysterious illness in *Parzival,* the semistarved and neglected girls of Lowood caught the infection: forty-five of the eighty were ill and there were many deaths. Miss Temple, one of the few kind teachers at the school, dedicated her every hour to caring for the sick, literally living with them night and day without respite. Helen, who was Jane's gentle and self-sacrificing friend, did not fear death. On the contrary, she told Jane shortly before her demise, "By dying young, I shall escape great suffering." Although disconsolate at her loss, Jane for the first time in her life understood what it meant to feel deep affection for someone. Never before had she loved or been loved.

Once the typhus epidemic had abated, an investigation was made into the school's environment and location by the religious authorities in whose care the destitute young ladies had been awarded. The site was declared unhealthy, the quality and quantity of food inadequate, the fetid and brackish water used in its preparation intolerable, and the students' clothing and accommodations wretched. Reverend Brocklehurst was dismissed from his directorship of the institution, and Miss Temple appointed in his stead. Lowood was then relocated on healthier ground, a more suitable building replaced the old and decaying one, and more humane and progressive regulations were instituted. Miss Temple transformed Lowood into a first-rate school.

Jane, who thrived in the new atmosphere, remained there as a student for six years and as a teacher for two. Not only did Miss Temple fill the void left by Helen's death, but became mother, advisor, and companion to her. Only after Miss Temple married a clergyman and left for a distant country did Jane decide it was time to leave Lowood. To continue living in a cloistered *home* environment, which Lowood was for Jane, would prevent her from learning, maturing, and functioning independently in the outside world.

Unlike the closed and covered window at Gateshead, the window at Lowood towards which Jane walks opens onto the world beyond. Having advertised for a post as governess—offering her

expertise in English, French, drawing, and music as an induce-
ment—she received an invitation from Mrs. Fairfax to come to
Thornfield Hall.

"Now at Last in Safe Haven"

Jane was psychologically prepared to step out of her home environment. She had become more independent, self-possessed, and
self-confident. A thinking type, she had learned to ponder and
analyze most of her acts and their possible repercussions on herself and others. Such methodical ways, though they protected her
somewhat from the vagaries of life had, by the same token, con-
siderably repressed her *feeling* world.

Upon entering Thornfield Hall and meeting the warm and understanding Mrs. Fairfax who ran the home during the protracted
absences of its owner, Mr. Rochester, Jane breathed a sign of relief: "I was now at last in safe haven." Her tasks as governess to
the eight-year-old Adele, Mr. Rochester's ward, were not overbur-
dening. Adele, the illegitimate daughter of one of Mr. Rochester's
"flighty" French mistresses who had since died, responded ac-
tively to Jane's ways, knitting a bond between the two, and although the child loved only dance, singing, and apparel, progress
in the educational field was soon forthcoming.

Thornfield Hall was a three-story high "stately and imposing"
mansion that Jane likened to a gentleman's manor house with "bat-
tlements round the top," giving it a picturesque look. Although
the uninhabited, dark, and eerie third story fascinated Jane, perhaps because of the many antique relics stored there, she sensed a
strangeness about the area: the tightly locked black doors, the
small winding staircase leading to the attic, the trapdoor opening
onto the roof, were all reminiscent of Bluebeard's castle. Some
mystery, she intuited, hidden away in the remoteness of this dismal space, was accentuated whenever "the pallid gleam of moonlight" poured through its tiny windows. On several occasions, as
she descended from the attic, Jane heard a loud, "tragic," "preternatural" laugh emanating from one of the rooms. Her dread
was soon assuaged by Mrs. Fairfax, who told her it was the seamstress, Grace Poole, who was making the sound. Jane's discomfiture was aroused on other occasions, when "eccentric murmurs"
coupled with strident tonalities emanated from the attic.

Architectural constructs, with their hidden chambers and pris-
ons, were played up by Gothic novelists for their horror, violence,
and supernatural effects. Such eeriness is not only a literary strategy, but has psychological import as well. Thornfield Hall, as a
building and spatial creation, may be viewed as the outer garment
of a secretive and vital inner system. Within the walls, columns,
ceilings, chimneys, attics, windows, turrets, and other structural
elements in Thornfield Hall exists a world in itself that may be
characterized as a microcosm or an expression of a preexistent
form that may be apprehended on a personal and temporal as
well as a transpersonal and atemporal level.

The silence and calm that reigned in Thornfield Hall, although
greatly appreciated at first, made Jane restless and agitated after a
few days. She enjoyed, however, walking through the mansion
garden, observing the "low-gliding and pale beaming sun" the
wild roses, blackberries, the evergreens, hawthorns, and hazel
bushes. On one occasion, while enjoying the view of hilltops and
dales all about and listening to the "thin murmurs" of forest life,
she suddenly heard a rude noise, like a metallic clatter, then saw
on the ground a fallen horse and its master. Jane rushed to the
man, helping him up as best she could and riveting her attention
on something arresting in the man's demeanor and eyes. After a
few short words of thanks, the stranger remounted his horse and
continued on his way. Jane was more than surprised when she
met the same man at Thornfield Hall the following evening. It
was Mr. Rochester.

On the rare occasions that Jane and Adele were called into Mr.
Rochester's presence, she felt his "dark, irate, and piercing" eyes
searching her face. Although she could not pinpoint the exact nature of her fascination for Mr. Rochester, she sensed something
mystifying and haunting about him. He, in turn, was impressed
by the young lady, so puritanical and forthright in her manner.
When he learned that Jane painted, he expressed a desire to see
some of her work.

Painting and drawing were crucial to Jane's well-being. Because
art forms enabled her to see "with the spiritual eye," they opened
her up to new worlds that transcended the thinking principle; they
were like a bridge between inner and outer spheres. No longer
bound to a three-dimensional world, Jane depersonalized phe-
nomena when painting, giving collective form and color to grip-
ping personal experiences. Only via the medium of art could she

fathom what was hidden from view and concretize what had vanished beneath the horizon of the rational world.[6]

The three watercolors Jane showed Mr. Rochester may be examined by way of exploration of their meanings as symbolic bearers of her most secret world.

The first represented clouds low and livid, rolling over a swollen sea: all the distance was in eclipse; so, too, was the foreground; or, rather, the nearest billows, for there was no land. One gleam of light lifted into relief a half-submerged mast, on which sat a cormorant, dark and large, with wings flecked with foam; its beak held a gold bracelet, set with gems, that I had touched with as brilliant tints as my palette could yield, and as glittering distinctness as my pencil could impart. Sinking below the bird and mast, a drowned corpse glanced through the green water; a fair arm was the only limb clearly visible, whence the bracelet had been washed or torn.

That Jane gave form to forgotten or repressed memories allowed her to loosen up what had been rigid and incarcerated within subliminal spheres. If one examines her paintings as projections of her continuous inner pulsations transmuted in understandable images, one may view them as a means of encouraging her to face certain irrational factors within her psyche. Although an artist's ego frequently depicts stereotypes—and Jane's painting is no exception, with its "low clouds" and "swollen sea"—it also reflects her personal psychological situation, as attested to by her blotting out of far-off space ("all the distance was in eclipse"). Her future, as well as her immediate present may then be viewed as confused, nebulous, ill-defined, and missing. Only the past serves as a modicum of security. That the clouds, identified with the spirit, are active, indicates a condition of turbulence in her values associated with religion and its moral ramifications; and the sea, identified with the instinctual sphere, being "swollen," suggests having inner pulsations. The nonexistent land or terra firma underscores perplexity and unsettling sensations due to the dichotomy between heaven and earth. That a "gleam of light" illuminates a "half-submerged mast," that part of a boat that serves to direct a ship's orientation, suggests directional confusion. The boat, so frequently a symbol for a person, is now rudderless and unable to follow its course. Although birds in general are identified with spiritual factors, the cormorant has the additional attribute of being a good diver. Perched on the mast, it has not only found temporary asylum, but it becomes an active participant in the probing or diving process, thus helping to catch the fish or those inner riches existing within the collective unconscious. The drowned corpse sinking into the waters suggests a whole unused, repressed, and dormant instinctual sphere that has slipped into oblivion. That the arm alone is visible indicates the existence of some element of *livingness* in the corpse: the arm still seeks to reach out and grasp onto life. Jane is at a crossroads: if she continues to allow her mind to guide her entire world, she will divest her existence of all feeling, thus becoming rigid, like the corpse in the picture.

The second watercolor transmutes even more accurately the outside world in terms of Jane's inward experience. It

contained for foreground only the dim peak of a hill, with grass and some leaves, slanting as if by a breeze. Beyond and above spread an expanse of sky, dark-blue as at twilight: rising into the sky was a woman's shape to the bust, portrayed in tints as dusk and soft as I could combine. The dim forehead was crowned with a star; the lineaments below were seen as through the suffusion of vapour; the eyes shone dark and wild; the hair streamed shadowy, like a beamless cloud torn by storm, or by electric travail. On the neck lay a pale reflection like moonlight; the same faint lustre touched the train of thin clouds from which rose and bowed this vision of the Evening Star.

While the first painting had been descensional, the second is ascensional. Hills and mountains, usually symbols of transcendence, indicate a need to find some common denominator between heaven and earth, inner and outer realms. Jane's pronounced asceticism and puritanism forever reject and obliterate her visceral approach to life. Unconsciously, she is trying to synthesize the polarization of tendencies within her psyche, which accentuate her distress. That grass, leaves, and a breeze are depicted on the hill suggests activity or a dynamic quality awaiting transformation. The image of a woman's body "rising into the sky" like an epiphany is another concrete manifestation of Jane's emotional needs. Her tendency is to spiritualize everything attached to the sexual world rather than experiencing it as a natural process. That the tints are soft underscores a need to fill a nonmaterial or aerated dimension and to flee into some ascensional realm, as well as an inability to focus on the physical side of life. That a star crowns the woman's forehead further underscores the celestial quality of Jane's yearnings. As a beacon and directional device, the evening star also affirms her desire to shed light on the world lying in darkness surrounding the brilliant glimmers of light. Although she would like to see into the forms depicted, her vision is blocked by vapor, reminiscent of the clouds in the previous painting. The eyes combined with the image of hair, analogized to a "beamless cloud" in a state of eruption, emphasizes once again her own confused and fragmented inner state.

The third painting

showed the pinnacle of an iceberg piercing a polar winter sky: a muster of northern lights reared their dim lances, close serried, along the horizon. Throwing these into distance, rose, in the foreground, a head—a colossal head, inclined towards the iceberg, and resting against it. Two thin hands, joined under the forehead, and supporting it, drew up before the lower features a sable veil; a brow quite bloodless, white as bone, and an eye hollow and fixed, blank of meaning, but for the glassiness of despair, alone were visible. Above the temples, amidst wreathed turban folds of black drapery, vague in its character and consistency as cloud, gleamed a ring of white flame, gemmed with sparkles of a more lurid tinge. This pale crescent was "the likeness of a kingly crown"; what it diademed was "the shape which shape had none."

That an iceberg emerges from a congealed, fixed, virtually empty landscape, indicates the extent of solidification or immobilization of potentialities that might emerge from Jane's vast and austere depths. The colossal head points up the emphasis she places on living exclusively in the mind; that it looks at and rests against an iceberg, confirms the rigidity and fixity of her approach to life. Constraint, control, austerity, and restrictive manners divest her of all naturalness, vivacity, and variety. The arm, indicating a desire to grasp onto some living entity, was the only visible limb in the first picture; it is now replaced by two thin hands resting under the forehead, suggesting that the support of a cerebral view of life is less significant. Although the woman in the picture is still pallid and bloodless, her heart virtually frozen over and no longer able to pump blood, life has not yet been subverted. It still exists within the white flame and the sparkling gems, waiting to be renewed and revitalized.

When Rochester asks Jane whether she was happy when she painted these pictures, her answer replicates the ambiguity of the forms depicted in the paintings: "I was absorbed, sir: yes, and I was happy." Intuitive by nature, Mr. Rochester knew only too well that a whole undeveloped realm existed within Jane. As for Jane, although growing increasingly fond of Mr. Rochester, she found his character "changeful and abrupt." Only when he began confiding to her segments of his past, his loves and losses, his inability to find happiness, his constant need for travel, gamble, debauchery, and escape did she begin to understand his sorrow, loneliness, disappointment, and melancholia that concluded each of his escapades. Jane suggested to him that only via thoughtful acts would he succeed in wiping away such self-indulgent and immoral habits and find fulfillment.

Their conversations, although taking a steadily more profound and intimate cast, were paradoxically stilled, but also intensified, by "a marrow-freezing incident." Late one evening Jane was suddenly awakened from sleep by a vague murmur in the gallery outside her door, followed by a "demoniac laugh-low, suppressed, and deep-uttered," then by gurgling and moaning tones and sounds of steps retreating into the gallery and third-story staircase. Terror struck her so deeply that she felt compelled to discover the root of the disturbance. As she stepped out of her door she saw smoke emanating from Mr. Rochester's room. Rushing in she saw that "tongues of flame darted round the bed: the curtins were on fire." He was in such a deep sleep that shaking him failed to rouse him. Jane found herself forced to pour a basin of water on and around him, thus quenching the flames. She finally awakened him. Mr. Rochester's gratitude toward her was such that he began alluding to her as his "cherished preserver," begging her, however, to say nothing of the incident and blaming Grace Poole for everything.

Deeply disturbed and puzzled by Mr. Rochester's secrecy, Jane's agitation, tinged with jealousy, reaches a new high when she discovers that her master has left Thornfield Hall and is to return with a group of high livers. One of the guests is the beautiful Blanche Ingram who, Jane is now informed, is to be married to Mr. Rochester. Witnessing Mr. Rochester's courtship of Miss Ingram and the latter's seductive responses, Jane struggles to accept the fact that she herself is plain and poor, and therefore of no interest to Mr. Rochester. Reason and discipline, the tools of volition, guide her in expressing her inner feelings.

To assuage the intensity of her inner struggle, Jane again has recourse to painting and sketching. She understands the therapeutic value of the artistic process of transforming pain into visual configurations and color tones. Through painting and drawing she brought unformed dynamic energies into visible configurations and dispositions. Thus did she liberate in part the chaos—caused by the great imponderables facing her and the loss of Mr. Rochester's interest—fomenting in her subliminal sphere. She directed her mind to execute two miniature portraits: one, a "Portrait of a Governess, disconnected, poor, and plain"; the other, the most beautiful face she had ever seen: that of Miss Ingram.

The two portraits, used as mnemonic devices, would be crucial in Jane's disciplinary ritual. Henceforth, whenever prone to sadness, she forced herself to compare the pictures: one of an exquisitely beautiful young girl, Mr. Rochester's intended; and the other of an "indigent, and insignificant plebeian." Such objectivity and adroit reasoning would not only keep her on course, but by eliminating all hope, would make her feel better.

Although relative security had returned to Jane's feeling world, turmoil continued to churn, spurred by recurring mysterious incidents. The moon, at certain times, seemed to prelude such strange events that Jane in some way identified with this celestial body, which she also personified. The image of the *moon*, associated with woman because of its periodic phases and curved contours, signals the presence of a whole preternatural dimension. Concealed behind its camouflage of purity and beauty it has its destructive side. Since antiquity, the moon has been identiried with Hecate, the Greek goddess of the underworld, ghosts, and sorcery, whose demons search for sacrificial victims to assuage her appetite. Also hidden behind the whiteness of its lunar rays is the moon's power to provoke storms and unrest of all kinds, and even dementia (the Latin word for moon, *luna*, and lunacy).

That Jane is awakened by moon rays prepares readers for a spine-tingling interlude: a savage, sharp, and shrill cry emanates from the attic, then "Help! help! help!" uttered three times. Moments later, Mr. Rochester calls Jane to help him. They make their way to the attic, where Jane sees the semiconscious Mr. Mason, one of the houseguests, bleeding profusely from a knife wound. Awaiting the arrival of the surgeon called in by Mr. Rochester, Jane hears a snarling, snatching sound, "almost like a dog quarrelling." The patient is finally removed from Thornfield Hall before the other guests awaken, leaving Jane in a quandary.

"Presentiments are strange things! and so are sympathies; and so are signs," Jane thinks. Understandably, after such an incident, nightmares begin to oppress her. One, in particular, concerned an infant she was cradling in her arms, dandling on her knee, and watching at play amid the daisies on a lawn. Seemingly charming, this dream was anxiety provoking for Jane because she had always identified children with ominous events, projecting onto them her own unhappy years spent at the Reed home. When identified, psychologically, with the ego, they represented, for her, dependence. Jane's ego, as that of the child, was still weak in certain areas, particularly with regard to men. The few male figures who had entered her world had been negative forces: John Reed and Reverend Brocklehurst had taunted and persecuted her; Mr. Lloyd, the apothecary, on the other hand, was kind and understanding. Although Mr. Rochester was still an enigma, she understood that since he was to wed Miss Ingram, she would have to leave Thornfield Hall. She was, indeed, a helpless infant, dependent upon someone else for survival, and she was fearful for her future.

Each time Jane is faced with a difficult decision, and each time she has found herself at a crossroad, the premonitory *child dream* emerges as a warning signal. The night she had been awakened by the bloodcurdling cry at Thornfield hall she had also dreamt of an infant. The present dream preceded the arrival of a messenger informing her of her Aunt Reed's imminent death and the elderly lady's wish to see her. Jane left immediately for her aunt's home. Unforgiving until the end, Mrs. Reed confessed to having lied to Jane's rich paternal and childless uncle whose existence was unknown to Jane. When inquiring about his niece's whereabouts, Mrs. Reed informed him that the young girl was dead. Forgiving always, Jane told her not to concerned, she would write him directly to tell him she was alive.

Upon her return to Thornfield Hall, Jane began making plans to leave. She then learned to her surprise that Mr. Rochester had decided not to wed Miss Ingram, and, when he proposed to Jane, she was simply incredulous. Now, for the first time, she allows her warmth and feeling world, until now so deeply closeted within her, to emerge.

The happy disbelief and excitement that Jane experienced during the busy month of courtship, which included the preparation of a trousseau, reached an extremely high pitch, yet she suffered moments of anxiety, as, for example, when she "faced the wreck of a chest-nut tree" blown down after a thunderous wind.

> It stood up, black and riven: the trunk split down the centre ... The cloven halves were not broken from each other, for the firm base and strong roots kept them unsundered below; though community of vitality was destroyed—the sap could flow no more: their great boughs on each side were dead, and next winter's tempest would be sure to fell one or both to earth: as yet, however, they might be said to form one tree—a ruin, but an entire ruin.

Jane put great stock in the destruction of a tree for its real as well as symbolical import. Because of the tree's verticality, it has been associated with the world axis. In that the tree links what is disparate—its roots digging into the depths of the earth (the underworld), its trunk on the ground (empirical existence) and its branches reaching heavenward (the celestial sphere) it becomes a premonitory image of a split or deep break about to occur in Jane's life.

As the wedding day approaches, Jane is "seized with hypochondriac foreboding" and another child-dream unfolds,

> that Thornfield Hall was a dreary ruin, the retreat of bats and owls. I thought that of all the stately front nothing remained but a shell-like wall, very high and very fragile-looking. I wandered, on a moonlight night, through the grass-grown enclosure within: here I stumbled over a marble hearth, and there over a fallen fragment of cornice. Wrapped up in a shawl, I still carried the unknown little child: I might not lay it down anywhere, however tired were my arms—however much its weight impeded my progress, I must retain it. I heard the gallop of a horse at a distance on the road; I was sure it was you; and you were departing for many years, and for a distant country. I climbed the thin wall with frantic, perilous haste, eager to catch one glimpse of you from the top: the stones rolled from under my feet, the ivy branches I grasped gave way, the child clung round my neck in terror, and almost strangled me: at last I gained the summit. I saw you like a speck on a white track, lessening every moment. The blast blew so strong I could not stand. I sat down on the narrow ledge; I hushed the scared infant in my lap: you turned an angle of the road: I bent forward to take a last look; the wall crumbled; I was shaken; the child rolled from my knee, I lost my balance, fell, and woke.

That Thornfield Hall is a ruin suggests an architectural metaphor for an inner psychic climate of fear and crushing despair at

Jane's inability to understand fully her future husband's character. She senses an inauthenticity about Mr. Rochester. Too many secrets, too many unanswered questions remain. Nor is her relationship with Mr. Rochester free flowing: a facade exists between them. Although he is loving and tender, his outer structure prevents her from penetrating inside the man. Is there an inside? she may wonder. Or has it been so worn, so mishandled, so mutilated that it has deteriorated and cannot be salvaged from decay and ruin?

Although the second part of Jane's dream finds her carrying a child she does not even know, and though she is burdened, she will not, for moral reasons, leave it. Such an image indicates that she is again projecting her ego and her weak and dependent sense of identity onto the lonely and helpless infant. The sudden appearance of a horse, representing that whole unlived instinctual and sexual part of herself, may be associated with Mr. Rochester, whom she had met when he had been thrown from a horse. Did she fear, unconsciously, that she, too, might be thrown down from the newfound heights she is soon to enjoy as the future Mrs. Rochester? Yet, though danger lies ahead, the figure in the dream is determined to climb the loosely constructed high wall in front of her, thus reaching the apogee of all her expectations. Predictably, the stones give way, the wall crumbles, indicating a breakdown of whatever security she had known and a disintegration of former values. The wall, representing rigorous asceticism and logical and reasonable procedures, had served her in good stead until now, though it, like all walls, separated her from the earth or instinctual sphere. Now that the wall has given way, she loses her balance, the child who had clung to her so desperately, almost strangling her, falls, indicating that the very object leading to her joy could also lead to her destruction. Everything that had steadied her until now—the right mental structures she had erected in her mind for future activities and her analytical procedures that had become her ego's mainstay were no longer operational.

Later that same night, Jane awakens to another harrowing sight: "a woman, tall and large, with thick and dark hair hanging long down her back" had entered her room, donned Jane's wedding veil, and was looking into the mirror. After removing the wedding veil moments later, this "fearful and ghastly" purple-lipped woman retreated to the door, but not before walking towards Jane to thrust her candles and her lurid face close to hers. Jane fainted. Upon regaining consciousness, she wondered whether she had experienced a dream or a hallucination and whether this apparition was a ghost or a vampire. Looking down to the floor, she saw her wedding veil torn from top to bottom. She had not been dreaming.

Doing his best to reassure Jane, Mr. Rochester insists that the wedding take place as planned, but just before the final vows, Mr. Mason, the man who had been knife-stabbed, reappears to inform everyone in the church that Rochester has a wife. Returning to Thornfield Hall Rochester takes Jane to the attic where his mad Jamaican wife, Bertha, Mr. Mason's sister, has been living in confinement. He then fills in the last details of his past. His father, in keeping with the laws of primogeniture, had bequeathed his entire fortune to his older brother and sent Mr. Rochester to the West Indies. It was there that he married Bertha, thinking she was a wealthy native. Unbeknown to Mr. Rochester, insanity ran in Bertha's family and shortly after their wedding her mind became completely disordered. Following the death of Mr. Rochester's father and brother, he brought Bertha back to Thornfield Hall. Now he begs Jane to live with him as his mistress, but although the idea attracts her, she realizes that the relationship would be morally untenable for her. She flees Thornfield at night.

"The awful passage"

After Jane's sudden departure, with but a few pence, and no distinction, she will again have to live out another "awful passage," overcoming, physically and psychologically, the obstacles in her path. Another initiation awaits her: experiencing starvation and homelessness, Jane sleeps in the woods, begs for food from door to door, and meets continuous rebuff. Not her fellow creatures, but only "universal mother, Nature" offered her comfort and hope: "I will seek her breast and ask repose." After sleeping in the Great Mother's arms, her hopes renewed, Jane makes her way to the home of Reverend St. John Rivers and his two sisters, who tend her convalescence. Warmed by the gentleness of the Rivers family, Jane accepts a post found for her by the reverend as director of a village school for the poor where she performs well and is reconciled to her new life.

Although Jane enjoys the company of the reverend's two sisters, she considers their brother a domineering and devouring force—an ascetic of the most rigid kind. His goal in life is to become a missionary and go to India where he will spread Christ's message. He asks Jane to be his wife, not because he loves her, but as his partner in Christ. When she refuses to marry him, but accepts to go with him as a savior of souls, he answers: "You shall be mine: I claim you—not for my pleasure, but for my Sovereign's service." Jane counters: "God did not give me my life to throw away."

The discovery that Jane Eyre is not only the Rivers' cousin, but that she is heiress to her paternal uncle's legacy, encourages the reverend to ask Jane to be his wife in the service of God. Unyielding and intransigent up to now, Jane, so vulnerable after her utter disappointment in marriage, is nearing the point of acquiescing, when suddenly she hears Mr. Rochester's voice calling her name three times. "I am coming!" she responds—"Wait for me!"

The telepathic or parapsychological event Jane has just experienced cannot be explained in a normal rational manner, that is, in keeping with Newton's established theory of causality, which posits that everything within the universe has causal explanations. C. G. Jung, on the other hand, posits acausality, in the belief that a factor mediates between the apparent incommesurability of body and psyche, and that it is this element that endows matter with a kind of "psychic" faculty, and psyche with a sort of "materiality." Each is able to influence the other because, as Jung points out, "living matter has a psychic aspect, and the psyche a physical aspect." It may be stated that reality in general is "grounded on an as yet unknown substrate possessing material and at the same time psychic qualities." If physical and psychic matter are linked, then acausal correspondences link psychic and physical events. Jung wrote:

It might be that psyche should be understood as *unextended intensity* and not as a body moving with time. One might assume the psyche gradually rising from minute extensity to infinite intensity, transcending for instance the velocity of light and thus irrealizing the body. In the light of this view the brain might be a transformer station, in which the relative infinite tension or intensity of the psyche proper is transformed into perceptible frequencies or "extensions." Conversely, the fading of introspective perception of the body explains itself as due to a gradual "psychification," i.e., intensification at the expense of extension. Psyche-light intensity in the smallest space.[7]

Should its frequency slacken to the speed of light, or less, the psychological projection could be observed by the human eye. The brain "tunes down the intensity of the psyche until it becomes bound to lower frequencies," which are then interpreted according to one's empirical understanding. What may be considered an impossibility (a parapsychological experience) becomes realizable in another domain that transcends empirical logic. The mind is considered a mediating force, a kind of computer that reduced high-frequency-energy intensity to lower levels, which the brain can then translate into an understandable language.[8]

It is on the basis of Jane's parapsychological experience that she rushes back to Thornfield hall to find it razed by fire, and learns that Mr. Rochester was blinded and maimed trying to save his wife, who had started the inferno and then jumped from the roof of the mansion to her death.

The *fire* as symbol reinforces the high-energy charges at work within the inhabitants remaining at Thornfield Hall: Bertha, whose anger, hatred, rage, and urge to kill predominates, and Mr. Rochester, whose bitterness mounts at the loss of his treasured Jane. Although light is considered an illuminating factor, it also sears and destroys. In Bertha's case, the intensity of the powerful electric charges in her brain became so chaotic as to have reached havocking proportions. Rochester's blindness, on the other hand, forces him to live inwardly.

The blinded Mr. Rochester, whose crushed hand had been amputated, now lives at Ferndean Manor, his other home. It is there that Jane seeks him out. In no way do his physical handicaps diminish their utter rapture. They marry and, after two years of bliss, partial vision returns to Rochester. Jane describes their firstborn as having inherited his father's "large, brilliant, and black eyes." As for Jane, she confessed: "No woman was ever nearer to her mate than I am: ever more absolutely bone of his bone and flesh of his flesh."

Jane Eyre, a tightly and minutely structured novel, not only dramatizes the struggles and challenges experienced by an orphan, both on the spiritual and sexual level, but brings the additional dimension to the narrative of an entire preternatural domain. Dreams, presentiments, and telepathic experiences are instruments used by the author to take readers out of empirical reality and lead them into transcendental spheres, where a whole spectral world lies buried beneath the visible and causal frame of reference.

What is also important and highly contemporary in *Jane Eyre* is the author's conviction that painting and drawing can be therapeutic. Not only do Jane's visual representations symbolize facets of her inner world, but they give her clues to the dangers that may lie ahead for her. A nonverbal and visual format, painting becomes a meditative device for Jane. Forms and silhouettes also indicate trouble that is brewing or happiness that lies in store, color tones create rhythmic patterns that catalyze energetic sequences on canvas, thus giving clues as to how to bridge and link certain actions in order to achieve a measure of safety and serenity.

The reviews for *Jane Eyre* were many and extraordinary. William Makepeace Thackeray, to whom Charlotte Brontë dedicated her novel, wrote: "It [*Jane Eyre*] interested me so much that I have lost (or won if you like) a whole day in reading it at the busiest period with the printers I know waiting for copy. . . . Give my respects and thanks to the author, whose novel is the first English one . . . that I've been able to read for many a day."[9]

Shirley: Social Realism, Feminism, and the Clergy

Although love motifs are interwoven into the plot of *Shirley,* Charlotte's novel, unlike the melodramatic *Jane Eyre,* is first and foremost a social commentary on the author's times. In that it is a record of the period, *Shirley* sometimes reads as sequences of panoramically chronicled events that rarely involve the reader. Written during the illnesses and deaths of Branwell, Emily, and Anne, *Shirley* is replete with subtly delineated and poignant autobiographical elements. Charlotte writes: "I cannot deny it was composed in the eager, restless endeavors to combat mental sufferings that were scarcely tolerable."[10] For this reason, perhaps, Charlotte chose not to have a personal relator carry events along, as in *Jane Eyre,* but to narrate through a third person, thus distancing himself from her story.

Shirley deals with the workers' movement in England and the adverse effect on it of the Napoleonic Wars. Although the thrust of the novel is the world of the cloth manufacturer and worker, other members of society—the clergy, the spinster, and the married woman—are also focused on. Impressive is Charlotte's extensive knowledge of the political, economic, historical, religious, and literary conditions in the England of her day.

Shirley is set in industrial England during the Luddite riots of 1811–12. These uprisings began when groups of textile workers, in the name of a mythical figure, King Ludd, destroyed knitting machines, cotton power looms, and wool-shearing machines, to which they attributed their unemployment or low wages. Poverty and discontent grew in the large urban populations as technological advances produced large-scale machinery requiring greater specialization.

Charlotte was familiar with the riots that took place in Yorkshire, and she handled her descriptions of such outbreaks masterfully, without glorifications or idealizations, and without moral or didactic connotations. Focusing on the inability of workers to feed their large families, she used incidents from *real* life, within the boundaries of good taste requied by her times. Suffering rather than romantic involvement was the material she used to build her story.

Social Realism

In *Shirley*, Charlotte may have wanted to make her imprint on the times by including descriptions of the impact on England of European turbulence. In 1848, the year prior to the publication of *Shirley*, liberal movements in France had caused riots to break out in Paris; rebellions in Italy fostered a rejection of Austrian Hapsburg occupation and despotism; demands for a constitutional monarchy, a free press, and other reforms were made by anti-Metternich groups in Germany; violent rioting occurred in Vienna, forcing Metternich's resignation; patriots in Bohemia and Hungary, taking advantage of the disarray within the Austrian Empire, also revolted, intent upon declaring national autonomy. 1848 was also the year in which Marx and Engels published their *Communist Manifesto* calling for the creation of a new socialism.

Charlotte was neither the first nor the last to be socially conscious of the physical and spiritual misery plaguing both Europe and England. Elizabeth Gaskell describes the conditions of the working classes in large industrial towns in Victorian England in her novel, *Mary Barton* (1848), while Charles Dickens's master-

fully detailed observations of streets and neighborhoods include
the foulest of haunts, the stench of starvation, and the horror of
sickness. Nor does Dickens omit scenes of overt cruelty toward
children and the helpless in such works as *Oliver Twist* (1837), *A
Christmas Carol* (1843), and *David Copperfield* (1850).

Charlotte's protagonist, Robert Gérard Moore, had moved
from his native Antwerp to the highly depressed region of Yorkshire, where he rented a mill. Realizing he faced imminent bankruptcy, he took measures, as had his competitors, that deprived
countless workers of their jobs. The countermeasures taken by la-
borers to fight starvation, disease, and eviction from their homes
and lands included the smashing of machinery and factories. In
Shirley, the rioters focus their ire on Hollow's Mill and, Robert,
its owner.

Robert's approach to his workers and their feelings toward him
are underscored by Charlotte not only to enhance the drama in
her novel but also for didactic reasons. An inveterate teacher, she
wants to familiarize her readers with the suffering plaguing England through attempts to activate social reform. The Reform Bill
(1832) championed by the Whig Party, alluding to themselves as
Liberals, favored the growing industrial middle class, but did little
for the workers. Agitation against starvation wages, unsanitary
conditions in the factories, and unemployment, gave birth to the
"People's Charter" movement (1838–48), which demanded,
among other reforms, universal suffrage and removal of property
qualifications. Although Chartism collapsed, it did pave the way
for some social legislation: the limiting of child labor in specific
industries, the abolition of ignominious workhouses, government
support of elementary education, and poor laws.

The orphaned Caroline Helstone, Reverend Helstone's niece,
and one of the protagonists in *Shirley*, is in love with Robert Gérard Moore. Although she understands little of his militance regarding his stand vis-à-vis his factory and its workers, she is
sensitive to the suffering of her fellow creatures and on many an
occasion attempts to point out to Robert the desperation to which
his economic policies have driven entire families. Materialism, the
basis of Robert's and society's values, has cut him off from his
feeling world. No matter how much she pleads with him, Robert,
a driven man, has but one goal: to make a success of his business.
Deciding to industrialize his mill even further, in total disregard
of his workers' rage and threats, Robert speaks in words both

potent and logical: "If I did as you wish me to do, I should be bankrupt in a month: and would my bankruptcy put bread into your hungry children's mouths?" To the threat of a burning down of the mill, Robert argues: "What then? . . . would that stop invention or exhaust science?—Not the fraction of a second of time! Another and better 'gig-mill' would rise on the ruins of this, and perhaps a more enterprising owner come in my place."

Outside of Caroline's all-consuming love for Robert, which she believes is unrequited, her days are dismal and void. Dominated in every way by her uncle, Reverend Helstone, a man determined to force women to retain the inferior status that has been their hallmark for centuries throughout Europe, the fate of Caroline, orphaned at an early age, is sealed.

Shirley Keeldar, whose name lands Charlotte's book its title, is unlike Caroline. Although orphaned as well, she is strong, outspoken, energetic, and independent. Heiress to the estate upon which Moore's mill stands, her goal is to enhance her property and thus make the most of her business acumen. The love given her by Mrs. Pryor, formerly her governess and now her companion, coupled with her personal wealth, beauty, and intelligence, endowed Shirley with the assurance necessary to develop inner strength and feelings of self-worth. Intelligent, well taught in business, she handles her own affairs. "The counting-house is better than my bloom-coloured drawing-room: I adore the counting-house." She works closely with Robert while also fulfilling her social commitments. "If men could see us as we really are, they would be a little amazed; but the cleverest, the acutest men are often under an illusion about women; they do not read them in a true light: they misapprehend them, both for good and evil." Shirley is a feminist, unwilling to accept the traditional role meted out to women, and rejecting any thought of male superiority. She also has heart, engaging as she does in parish affairs, particularly the struggle between employers and employers. Because she works closely with Robert and has little time to devote to Caroline, the passive maiden is convinced that the two are in love.

The Clergy

From the very outset of *Shirley*, readers are aware of the divergent views of the clergy with regard to workers, feminism, and their own religious orientation. The most unfeeling of them all is the intransigently conservative Tory, Reverend Helstone, who sends his curate, Malone, to help Robert defend his property.

When dealing with starving workers, ailing parishioners, or dissenters of any type, curates—Malone and others of his ilk, such as Donne and Sweeting, as depicted by Charlotte—seem oblivious to what has been termed "Christian compassion." A sample of the author's unforgettable satire of the clergy and their gluttonous, scheming, hypocritical, and hard-hearted natures follows:

These gentlemen are in the bloom of youth; they possess all the activity of that interesting age—an activity which their moping old vicars would fain turn into the channel of their pastoral duties, often expressing a wish to see it expended in a diligent superintendence of the schools, and in frequent visits to the sick of their respective parishes. But the youthful Levites feel this to be dull work; they prefer lavishing their energies on a course of proceeding, which, though to other eyes it appear more heavy with ennui, more cursed with monotony, than the toil of the weaver at his loom, seems to yield them an unfailing supply of enjoyment and occupation. What attracts them [to themselves] . . . is not friendship; for whenever they meet they quarrel. It is not religion; the thing is never named amongst them: theology they may discuss occasionally, but piety—never. . . . Mr. Sweeting is mincing the slice of roast-beef on his plate, and complaining that it is very tough; Mr. Donne says the beer is flat. . . . "More bread!" cries Mr. Malone. . . . Mr. Malone's father termed himself a gentleman; he was poor and in debt, and besottedly arrogant; and his son was like him. . . . The curates had good appetites, and though the beef was "tough," they ate a great deal of it. They swallowed, too, a tolerable allowance of the "Flat beer," while a dish of Yorkshire pudding, and two tureens of vegetables, disappeared like leaves before locusts. The cheese, too, received distinguished marks of their attention; and a spice-cake which followed by way of dessert, vanished like a vision, and was no more found.

The curates, meantime, sat and sipped their wine; a liquor of unpretending vintage, moderately enjoyed. Mr. Malone, indeed, would much rather have had whisky; but Mr. Donne, being an Englishman, did not keep the beverage. While they sipped, they argued; not on politics, nor on philosophy, nor on literature—these topics were now as ever totally without interest for them—not even on theology, practical or doctrinal; but on minute points of ecclesiastical discipline, frivolities which seemed empty as bubbles to all save themselves.

The spiritual welfare of Reverend Helstone's parishioners is far from being his first priority; he prefers a good fight with his disparagers. Dr. Boultby's never-ending platitudes are also a butt of Charlotte's ire. The single celibate priest of the group, he is perhaps the only prelate interested in his parishioners, but his interest focuses mainly on women parishioners.

Despite the clergy's wrongs, in no way does Charlotte discard Christianity. "Let England's priests have their due: they are a faulty set in some respects, being only of common flesh and blood, like us all; but the land would be badly off without them: Britain would miss her church, if that church fell. God save it! God also reform it!"

Feminism

Reverend Helstone is one of the most outrageous and regressive antifeminists in all of Charlotte's writings. She takes him to task in the most outspoken and direct manner possible, condemning him for his lack of compassion and humanitarianism as well as his injustices. Along with other men of the cloth, he is opposed to women's education, their free choice of a husband, and equal voice in government and in society.

As Reverend Helstone's ward, Caroline is allowed to do nothing but sew and read a few well-chosen books. In good Victorian tradition, she is brought up to hate and fear sexuality, and thus frequently, albeit unconsciously, longs for it. Because she is a woman and poor, Caroline cannot enter business; nor is she given permission to become a governess—the only profession for which she is suited. Although other options are open to Caroline—the job of household servant, for example—they are out of the question, given her guardian's status as prelate. Marriage, the best of her options, since she has no dowry, might throw her into the arms of a repugnant old man chosen by her guardian. There is, of course, spinsterhood. But such an alternative leaves her open to ridicule and isolation in a male-dominated society, and to the loneliness and emptiness of an existence spent dusting furniture and tending to houseplants, alleviated in part by a selfless devotion to a cause or to the sick. Such prospects must have made Caroline shudder.

Reverend Helstone's dogmatism is in keeping with the Pauline doctrine, which states God's desire that woman be subservient to man: therefore, women must live, if married as slaves and servants to their husbands and, if spinsters, to society. In the First

Epistle of Paul to Timothy one reads: "Let the woman learn in silence with all subjection. But suffer not a woman to teach, nor to usurp authority over the man, but to be in silence. For Adam was first formed, then Eve. And Adam was not deceived, but the woman being deceived was in the transgression" (2:10–14).

Forbidden to devote herself to a cause or to any kind of work outside the home, and feeling unloved by Robert, Caroline lives within herself—withdrawn in a lonely, silent world. As her desperation increases, she begins questioning her very reason for living. Because no answers are forthcoming, her dejection and passivity increase. She looks down on herself and her vacuous existence palls. Forever enclosed in her uncle's strict home environment or devoting herself to church affairs, Caroline not only becomes increasingly introverted, but unrelated to the world of reality. Her existence turns into a long reverie focusing on Robert and on his activities. Longing unconsciously for death, and weakened by loss of appetite, Caroline suddenly takes ill. Her malady? anorexia nervosa, due, as some of today's psychiatrists suggests, to a life devoid of *real* love, particularly from a mother or mother figure. Mrs. Pryor, Shirley's companion, aware of Caroline's precarious condition, asks Reverend Helstone if she may care for the young lady. No sooner does he acquiesce than Mrs. Pryor reveals to her patient that she is her mother, explaining that she had so feared Caroline's father that she had run away from him, leaving their infant daughter to his care. At the time, she had not thought of the possibility of his untimely death. Only now—and for the first time—is *real* love lavished on Caroline, thus healing her soul/psyche along with her body. When, at the end of *Shirley,* she marries Robert, her joy is complete and without conflict.

Shirley Keeldar, on the other hand, having been brought up by the loving Mrs. Pryor, is psychologically independent and in no way frightened of standing up to her Uncle Sympson, who would like her to marry a rich young man she does not love. Unbeknownst to everyone, Shirley is in love with and determined to marry Louis Moore, Robert's virtually penniless brother. In fighting her battle for independence of spirit and mind, Shirley experiences great inner conflict between her longing for Louis and her desire to remain her own guide. Like Caroline, her psychological tension also leads her to believe she is doomed to a fatal illness. Having been bitten by a rabid dog, she fears she will become a victim of madness and extracts Louis's promise that, in such a case, he would not only have her treated, but would administer a strong dose of narcotic to insure her speedy death. Shirley's fears, however, turn out to be unfounded.

Impressed by Shirley's strength of character, Louis, who had shied away from her because of the economic disparity between them, falls in love with her. What seems utterly out of character for Shirley is her about-face prior to her marriage to Louis. A feminist until this moment—strong in business and determined to remain independent—she now decides she wants a husband who will be stronger than she. "I prefer a *master*. . . . A man I shall feel it impossible not to love, and very possible to fear."

Louis, cognizant of her conflict and frustrated sexual urges, reacts to her change of mind and heart in an absurdly preposterous manner: "Pantheress!—beautiful forest-born!—wily, tameless, peerless nature! she gnaws her chain: I see the white teeth working at the steel! She has dreams of her wild woods, and pinings after virgin freedom."

After her marriage, Shirley's life focuses solely on her husband: "Her captor alone could cheer her; his society only could make amends for the lost privilege of liberty; in his absence, she sat or wandered alone; spoke little and ate less." One wonders whether, following the first few months of sexual fulfillment, she would not slowly meld the disparate views by returning to her socially committed work while still functioning as a loving and understanding wife. One role need not negate the other. Rather, each frequently complements the other.

Critics, particularly those who had been impressed with *Jane Eyre*, were not generous in their reviews of *Shirley*. G. H. Lewes wrote: "*Shirley* cannot be received as a work of art. It is not a picture; but a portfolio of random sketches for one or more pictures. . . . Currer Bell has much yet to learn,—and, especially, the discipline of her own tumultuous energies."[11] Laura L. Hinkley thought *Shirley* included too many themes—history, economics, ecclesiasticism, and personal destinies—for a cohesive whole to be maintained.[12] Jacob Korg, however, was impressed by Charlotte's application of "the romantic myth to the world of social realities. When used as an instrument of criticism, her passionate belief in nature and individualism took the form of a peculiar religion. Drawn from a mystic source, the reveries in which Shirley and Caroline undergo the experience of communion with the absolute, it is extended into everyday life to provide standards of conduct."[13]

Villette: A Nonstereotypic Fictional Biography

Villette (1853), more personal and more autobiographical than Shirley, dramatizes Charlotte's early traumatic years and particularly her Brussels experience. Villette, unlike The Professor, Jane Eyre, and Shirley, does not end on the happy note so representative of the stereotypic romantic fictional conclusions. Significant as well is the fact that Charlotte's protagonist, Lucie Snowe (she had first named her Lucy Frost because in "her veins ran ice"), apparently resembles her own attitude and temperament more closely than do any of her other heroines.[14]

A true Bildungsroman, Villette deals with the building of an orphan's personality as she fends through the harrowing drama that is her life. Whether in England, living with her widowed godmother, Mrs. Bretton, or working for a dour old invalid, Miss Marchant, or in Brussels teaching in a pensionnat for young ladies, Lucy struggled constantly against solitude, isolation, and ridicule.

Most spectacular in Villette was Charlotte's treatment of the multidimensional school environment from a variety of perspectives. Not only did the very building in which students and faculty were lodged take on a character and a life of its own, but it became a microcosm of the macrocosm. The interconnecting lives of the inhabitants of the establishment are observed by Charlotte as first person narrator as well as a third-person, all-seeing eye. The directress of the pensionnat for young lades, Madame Beck; the school's physician, Dr. John; the literature and drama teacher, Paul Emmanuel; and some of the students, such as the flighty and coquettish Ginevra Fanshawe—all are brought to life as unforgettable miniature portraits in a panoply of dramatic sequences. Never before had Charlotte captured so incisively and succinctly the thoughts, yearnings, and fears of a group as in Villette. Her protagonist's reactions to her stay in a foreign land, with its tongue, customs, culture, and religion are equally authentic. As a Protestant in a Catholic country, Charlotte's Brussels experience taught her the meaning of belonging to a minority group, and the problems and benefits associated therewith.

The Bildungsroman

Just as the Bildungsroman focuses on the development of an individual, good examples of which are Goethe's Wilhelm Meister's

Apprenticeship and Dickens's *David Copperfield*, so too does *Villette* discourse upon the evolution of a heroine in sequentially and nonsequentially organized events. Unlike the heroes of the Bildungsroman who usually fulfill themselves and their goals, Lucy Snowe, although succeeding in earning economic and intellectual independence, will know professional but not emotional satisfaction. As a Protestant, marriage to a Catholic husband would not have been acceptable and thus happiness could not even be envisaged. This literary quandry was resolved by causing Lucy's fiancé, Paul Emmanuel, who had been sent to the West Indies for three years to settle his family's estate, to drown at sea in a shipwreck during a violent storm.

Villette may be divided into two parts, the first dealing with Lucy's struggle to find a modus vivendi, and the second emphasizing Lucy's long bouts of despair, inertia, and mental illness as she struggles between her yearnings for love and the reality of her painfully lonely situation.

The reader first meets the fourteen-year-old Lucy Snowe when she is living with her godmother, Mrs. Bretton. The reader knows nothing of Lucy's parents or her background—only that she had been living with "kinsfolk." Although kindly disposed toward the young orphan, Mrs. Bretton is unemotional in temperament. Her sixteen-year-old warm and gentle son, Graham, is his mother's counterpart. Lucy's existence in Mrs. Bretton's household takes on the characteristics of a reportage as she observes and relates, in what she believes to be a relatively objective manner, her reactions to events and situations, when, in fact, they are the confessions of a highly vulnerable and deeply troubled individual.

One of the most moving incidents in *Villette* revolves around the stay of Polly Home at Mrs. Bretton's; Polly is a motherless child who is deeply attached to her father. Her despair upon being told that her father must leave for Europe on business moves Mrs. Bretton to a rare show of motherly feelings. Lifting the child into the window seat, she tells her to watch for her father who is to come to visit her one last time before leaving.

She had sat listlessly, hardly looking, and not counting, when—my eye being fixed on hers—I witnessed in its iris and pupil a startling transfiguration. These sudden, dangerous natures—*sensitive*, as they are called—offer many a curious spectacle to those whom a cooler temperament has secured from participation in their angular vagaries. The fixed and heavy

gaze swam, trembled, then glittered in fire; the small, overcast brow
cleared; the trivial and dejected features lit up; the sad countenance
vanished, and in its place appeared a sudden eagerness, an intense
expectancy.

When Mr. Home finally bids his last farewell to Polly, "she
dropped on her knees at a chair with a cry, 'Papa!' " and for
days, "the little creature . . . did for herself what none other could
do—contended with an intolerable feeling; and, ere, long in some
degree, repressed it."

Ironically, while recounting these and succeeding events, Lucy
prides herself on her ability to contend with her own emotion: "I,
Lucy Snowe, was calm." When, however, Polly begins transfer-
ring her love for her father onto Graham Bretton, and he, re-
sponding to her need, treats her with utmost gentleness and
sensitivity, inviting her to nestle in his arms, Lucy experiences
profound sorrow and jealousy. Her unconscious feelings of displacement, rejection, and pain may be measured in terms of Polly's increasingly dominant position in the household.

Unable to deal with what she considers her displacement from
a formerly favored position in the Bretton household, she refers to
Polly not by name, but by using the collective pronoun subject, *it*,
thus implying a profound identification with this suffering object.
Anger is also implicit in Lucy's relationship with Polly, as, for
example, when Lucy provokes Graham's rebuff of Polly, producing the sought-for devastating effect on Polly's psyche. Nevertheless, compassion is also part of Lucy's ambiguous and complex
nature. Called to join her father on the Continent, Polly trembles
with emotion at leaving her beloved Graham; Lucy invites the
child, with whom she shares a room, to come into her bed, and
readers become privy to Lucy's stifled capacity and need for tenderness and love. Gazing at Polly, she wonders how she would
ever "get through this world, or battle with this life? How will
she bear the shocks and repulses, the humiliations and desola-
tions, which books and my own reason tell me are prepared for
all flesh?"

A few weeks after Polly's departure from Mrs. Bretton's home,
Lucy returns to her "kinsfolk," where she remains for the next
eight years. The reader is given no details concerning her life during this interim period, except that her sleep was plagued by
nightmares, revolving mainly around tempests, shipwrecks, and

fear of being tossed overboard into the icy, briny waves where she would be left to perish.

Lucy is found next working as a nurse-companion for the elderly Miss Marchmont. Although living with this difficult cripple is distressing to her, she clings to her new surrogate mother, as gradually an understanding grows between them and the old lady decides to provide for Lucy's future. Before effecting her plan, however, Miss Marchmont dies and Lucy, a "pilgrim" once again, must do "war" with the world in order to carve out her niche.

A voice that may be identified with that heard by Abraham and Christ tells her to "leave this wilderness and go out hence." To where, she did not know. Because God was with her, she trusted Him and fear did not beset her. On the contrary, she felt energized by His presence, as she goes first to London, and then decides to board a ship to Brussels. Terror and thoughts of death take hold of her once she becomes aware of the planlessness of her peregrinations. "I thought of the Styx, and of Charon rowing some solitary soul to the Land of the Shades." So personal is her relationship with God that, despite her seasickness during the Channel crossing, she feels reassured and encouraged in her decision to leave England. Like Noah's venture during and after the Flood, she, too, perceives a rainbow as a sign of her covenant with Deity.

On shipboard, Lucy meets Ginevra Fanshawe, a student at Madame Beck's school for girls in Villette, Belgium. After disembarkation, Lucy, walking aimlessly about the dark streets of an alien town without knowing a word of French, miraculously finds herself in front of Madame Beck's *Pensionnat de Demoiselles,* where she equally miraculously is hired as nurse for Madame Beck's three children and in a matter of days promoted to English teacher.

Pensionnat as Microcosm

Madame Beck's school is a world in foment and torment. The names chosen by Charlotte for her novel, *Villette* (small city), for the school and its student body, Labassecour (from the French, *basse-cour,* meaning an inner farmyard court reserved for breeding chickens), and its location on Rue Fossette (dimple) suggest her rather low opinion of the place and its inhabitants. Self-righteous perhaps, she sees the school establishment as primitive, irrational, idle, and ignorant. Nor do the sexually starved young ladies harbored in Madame Beck's so-called protective establishment arouse her admiration: corruption, deception, and coquettishness reign. The students, however, are not always to blame for their ways: their comportment is a product of their rootless upbringing, most being shunted back and forth for one reason or for another from England to France, to Germany and back again to Brussels, by their parents or guardians. Ginevra Fanshawe, for example, who has spent so many years of her young life being shunted back and forth from one land to another, one boarding school to another, barely knows how to write her native tongue and her spelling and grammar leave much to be desired. As for her religious affiliation, she can barely tell the difference between Protestantism, Romanism, Lutheranism, or any other brand of Christianity.

Madame Beck is one of Charlotte's unforgettable creations. Ruling her kingdom like a dragon, she possesses an emotionless intensity, a subtlety, and an intransigence that leave her without smile or scowl. To maintain her school's prisonlike order, Madame Beck spies on the inmates, both students and faculty. Nothing is said or done within the establishment without her knowledge. Either at night when she thinks Lucy is asleep, or by day when she knows her to be occupied elsewhere, she meticulously examines her effects, counting the money in her purse, and making wax impressions of her keys. A fearsome figure in Lucy's eyes, she is depicted as a "Minos in petticoats," a "huntress" who works behind the scenes to gain her own ends. That bleakness and blackness dominate in Madame Beck's school in sharp contrast to the illuminated and fun-filled city outside, attests to its morbidly repressive ambiance.

Should any of Madame Beck's children or boarders fall ill, Dr. John is in attendance. Handsome and well-mannered, he speaks openly to Lucy of his love for the coquettish Ginevra. She, who enjoys having many suitors at her beck and call, unbeknownst to all, has eyes only for M. de Hamal, an international playboy type. In time, Lucy falls in love with John. Although he is kindly disposed toward her, Lucy's plain face, her social inferiority, and her overtly Puritanical ways deflect him from deeper attention. In a despondent mood, withdrawing into herself, she thinks: "Deeper than melancholy, lies heartbreak."

An interlude of no mean importance occurs when one of the students playing the male lead in a school play commemorating Madame Beck's birthday falls ill. A substitute must be found. Paul Emmanuel, the play's director, insists that Lucy fill in. She, determined to continue her reclusive mode of existence within the school confines, rejects the very thought of exhibiting herself before others. That she would have to play the role of a male lover—she who had repressed the very thought of sexuality—was unthinkable to her. After much cajoling and threats, Lucy finally submits to Paul's demands. After studying her part for several hours only, Lucy appears on stage transformed: her own unconscious masculine identity lends her the energy, power, and competitive spirit needed for the role. She, who had been passive, living out a shadow existence, was about to step out into the limelight as if she belonged there. In complete possession of her part and her actions, she was stunned by the very power of her vigor and by her success with the audience.

Guilt at having enjoyed the experience so intensely encourages Lucy to retire still further from activity and to turn inwards, toward what could be alluded to as her morbid abyss. Perhaps, she reasons, when in the throes of despondency, her agony is part of God's "great plan that some must deeply suffer while they live, and I thrilled in the certainty that of this number, I was one." Her ordeal not only weakens Lucy, but during her day hours of reverie and at night as well, her mind is flooded with dreams of terror and anxiety. She feels surrounded by beasts of prey, fierce and ravenous animals ready to pounce on her or awaiting her in ambush. Increasingly passive, she becomes victimized by her own solitary and loveless world. A voyeur, she observes, defines, rationalizes her every move and thought.

Matters reach a crisis during the summer months: students and faculty have vacated the school and Lucy remains virtually alone to care for a child suffering from Down's syndrome. One night, driven by terrifying feelings of alienation, Lucy suddenly rushes out of the school and wanders disoriented through the streets. Coming suddenly upon a Roman Catholic church, she enters and confesses to the priest, Father Silas, who seeks to convert her. Upon leaving the house of worship, Lucy collapses in the street and by chance is found unconscious moments later by Dr. John who is passing by. He takes her to his home where his mother— none other than Mrs. Bretton—cares for her. When Lucy recovers

consciousness, she recognizes Mrs. Bretton and realizes the incredible truth that Dr. John is none other than Graham Bretton.
She learns that mother and son had moved to Brussels because of
financial reverses.

Upon her return to Madame Beck's pension, Lucy awaits the
letters Doctor John had promised to write her. Intent upon maintaining utter secrecy, Lucy takes the first letter she receives to the
attic where she hopes to find peace and serenity. Instead, a ghost
dressed as a nun appears before her. Traumatized, she relates
the incident to Dr. John and Madame Beck. Both feel she has
been hallucinating.

Lucy falls desperately in love with Dr. John who sees in her a
kind and wonderful sister. One evening, when accompanying him
to the theater, a fire breaks out and he, the good samaritan that
he is, helps rescue a young woman who is about to be crushed by
a stampeding crowd. The young lady turns out to be none other
than the Polly whom Lucy and John had known as children. Having inherited a title, she is now called Paulina Mary, and her father, the Count de Bassompierre. Friendships are renewed and in
time Polly and Dr. John marry.

What Lucy had failed to realize was that after her stage performance Paul Emmanuel had fallen in love with her, which explained his irascibility, willfulness, and his temper tantrums.
Meanwhile, Lucy had also changed. Since her love for Dr. John
had been quelled, she views Paul Emmanuel in a different light. A
single, but virtually insurmountable obstacle stands in the way of
their love: Paul is a Roman Catholic and Lucy is a Protestant.

Protestantism versus Catholicism

Marriage between Lucy and Paul could not have taken place because Charlotte had not succeeded in resolving her profound fear
and distrust of Roman Catholicism. Within the school complex
itself, dominated by the corrupt and unfeeling directress, Madame
Beck, Lucy sensed the existence of a most circuitous and dishon-
est element buried beneath aesthetically appealing and loving holy
images and rituals: "The CHURCH strove to bring up her children
robust in body, feeble in soul, fat, ruddy, hale, joyous, ignorant,
unthinking, unquestioning."

When Lucy realized that her love for Dr. John was unrequited,
she also understood that she would have to remove herself from

Madame Beck's reach. She was prepared to accept suffering, not as something to be rejected and against which she would rebel, but as part of the Christian credo. No longer did Lucy struggle against what she had always interpreted as the Christian God's insensitivity, lack of compassion, and injustice. Rather, she now bathed in the serenity that comes with the acceptance of humankind's inability to dominate empirical events. To be aware of one's impotence, however, does not exclude the necessity of meeting life's obligations. She understood she must do her best to lead a moral and spiritual existence without anticipating any rewards.

Lucy had taken a giant step in her understanding of her own and humanity's earthly lot and focus. Whatever pain was meted out to her, she would no longer struggle to comprehend it or attempt to equate good deeds with happiness. What strengthened her determination not to convert was the theological work that Paul, at Father Silas's instigation, had placed in her desk. It sought not to appeal to the mind, but to feelings, luring converts into its fold with promises of "enjoying the unspeakable solace of praying [the dead] out of purgatory." Why didn't the author of the document dispense with purgatory altogether? Lucy wondered. Although she questioned the author's "rickety" judgment and insincerity, the volume, on the whole, "amused and did not painfully displease me. It was a canting, sentimental, shallow little book."

Of greatest significance to Lucy was Protestantism's respect for the Bible as an instrument of God. Lucy's conclusion is simple and pure, in keeping with the sanctity of her faith.

O lovers of power! O mitred aspirants for this world's kingdoms! an hour will come, even to you, when it will be well for your hearts, pausing faint at each broken beat, that there is a Mercy beyond human compassions, a Love stronger than this strong death which even you must face, and before it all; a Charity more potent than any sin, even yours; a Pity which redeems worlds—nay, absolves priests.

Although conceding errors in all creeds, the more Lucy is exposed to "Popery," the closer she clings to "Protestantism." She realizes

how severely pure was my own compared with her whose painted and meretricious face had been unveiled for my admiration. I told him how we kept fewer forms between us and god, retaining, indeed, no more than, perhaps, the nature of mankind in the mass rendered necessary or due observance. I told him I could not look on flowers and tinsel, on wax lights and embroidery, at such times and under such circumstances as should be devoted to lifting the secret vision to Him whose home is infinity and His being eternity; that when I thought of sin and sorrow, of earthly corruption, mortal depravity, weighty temporal woe, I could not care for chanting priests or mumming officials; that when the pains of existence and the terrors of dissolution pressed before me, when the mighty hope and measureless doubt of the future arose in view, *then* even the scientific strain, or the prayer in a language learned and dead, harassed with hindrance a heart which only longed to cry,— "God be merciful to me, a sinner!"

Paul finally understood Lucy's *act of faith* and respects her for it. That he had to die at sea so that his marriage to Lucy could not take place may imply a willed tragic ending on the surface; more likely, however, it indicates an inability on Charlotte's part to come to terms with Roman Catholicism: she feared its power and considered its emphasis on pomp and circumstance offensive to the purity and simplicity of Christ's teachings.

Villette, multifaceted in its spiritual, psychological, and cultural impact, is also rich in drama and character analysis. That it interweaves autobiographical elements, though reset and altered to suit the needs of the story line, lends greater authenticity and meaning to the author's reasoned thoughts and emotions. Because Charlotte wanted to write a true-to-life story, rejecting the conventions of the popular novelists of her day, some readers, including her publisher, George Smith, considered *Villette* lacking in unity of plot, overly fragmented. There were, to be sure, certain literary strategies and Gothicisms indulged in by Charlotte—the nun episode, the coincidences, the chance meetings—but these added to the novel's momentum, to its ferment, and the climate of mystery, terror, love, anxiety, and quietude imbricated into the work's textured sequences. Designed to keep the reader's interest highly pitched, movement throughout *Villette* follows a rhythmic pattern: it slackens and intensifies, depending on Lucy's engagement or nonengagement in the action. The detailed layout of the school, its rooms and anterooms, its various floors, and mazelike corridors, in addition to what may seem endless rounds of aimless discourse, are all interwoven with point into Charlotte's carefully planned work.

The critics were divided in their reactions to *Villette*. Harriet Martineau found it an "almost intolerably painful" work that never allowed the reader any "respite" from misery and the "atmosphere of pain [which] hangs about the whole." George Eliot considered *Villette* "a still more wonderful book than *Jane Eyre*. There is something almost preternatural in its power." Thackeray called it rather "vulgar" because its heroine fell in love with two men at once. G. H. Lewes thought of it as "a work of astonishing power and passion." Matthew Arnold castigated it: "Hideous, undelightful, convulsed, constricted . . . one of the most utterly disagreeable books I have ever read."[15]

It is unfortunate that Charlotte should be known for *Jane Eyre* alone, when *Shirley* and *Villette* are also such stunningly meaningful and powerful works.

Conclusion

We may ask ourselves where—if possible at all—to place the novels of the Brontë sisters? What traditions do they follow? What have they brought to literature? What is the mark they have left?

Let us turn back to eighteenth-century England and to the new and vigorous literary form—the novel—in the process of increasing in scope and breadth until its burgeoning a century later. Novels such as *Pamela* by Samuel Richardson (1740), *Tom Jones* (1749) by Henry Fielding, *Tristram Shandy* (1759–67) by Laurence Sterne, *Roderick Random* (1748) by Tobias Smollett, *The Vicar of Wakefield* (1764) by Oliver Goldsmith, drew accolades from readers and critics alike. Popular as well, but in sharp contrast to the domestic and rural narratives flooding the market, were the Gothic romances: bloodcurdling and terrifying mysteries taking place in secluded, haunted, labyrinthine castles. This genre reached its pinnacle with Ann Radcliffe's *The Mysteries of Udolpho* (1794) and Horace Walpole's *The Castle of Otranto* (1764), forerunners of the modern detective and horror story.

Extensive and intensive nineteenth-century novels broadened their themes, treating a variety of environments, characters, and ideologies. Women's narratives, such as *Evelina* (1778) by Fanny Burney and *Castle Rackrent* (1800) by Maria Edgeworth, paved the way for Jane Austen's *Sense and Sensibility* (1811) and *Pride and Prejudice* (1813). George Eliot's *The Mill on the Floss* (1860) and *Daniel Deronda* (1876) give evidence to her philosophical view that "Whatsoever a man soweth, that shall he also reap." Historical romances gained prominence with *Ivanhoe* (1819) and *Kenilworth* (1821) by Sir Walter Scott. Realistic tradition flourished during the Victorian age under the pen of Charles Dickens in such novels as *Oliver Twist* (1837–39) and *David Copperfield*

(1849–50). Acclaimed as well was *Vanity Fair* (1847–48) by William M. Thackeray.

Whereas Emily, Charlotte, and Anne Brontë followed to some extent English traditional modes, they were also pioneers in the novel form. Their exploration of subliminal realms, by subsuming dreams, signs, symbols, portents, preternatural experiences, yielded them untold riches with regard to the human personality. Champions of truth, they approached their tragic destinies rationally, combining individual and family needs with broader factors involving social commitments: rights of women, education, sanitation, help for the poor, rehabilitation, and the like.

Their writings, a source of joy as well as of self-knowledge, helped sustain them during their hours of sorrow and their cohabitation with death. Each probed her inner and outer worlds with vitality and sensitivity, courageously decanting personal feelings and needs in their novels and poems, but always tempered by reason, discipline, elegance of manner—and superb artistry. Their boldness of expression, when conveying their need of romance, their sense of morality, their highly principled views and religious principles, were equally overt and unmitigated when condemning what they disliked, such as the hypocrisy of so many men of the cloth. The authenticity and eloquence of their relationship to Nature in all of her moods was an added jewel in the creation of the unique organic structures that were their novels. Charlotte's statement concerning her creative impulses mirrors those made by her sisters: "Not one feeling on any subject, public or private, will I ever affect that I do not really experience."[1]

Immensely innovative in perception as well as in prosody, the Brontës' novels are in many ways analogous to the painter's dual creative modes described by John Constable:

In the one, by a careful application to what others have accomplished, the artist imitates their works or selects and combines their various beauties; in the other, he seeks excellence at its primitive source—nature. In the first he forms a style upon the study of pictures, and produces either imitative or eclectic art; in the second, by a close observation of Nature, he discovers qualities existing in her which have never been portrayed before, and thus forms style which is original.[2]

The same paths were taken by the Brontës when composing their carefully structured novels. Each conveys both a highly personal and collective vision of their protagonists' inner struggles; each invests in melodramatic intent to accentuate the story line, thus generating excitement and tension; each deploys subtle and obvious satire to condemn certain values foisted upon their characters by society in general and by a male-dominated world in particular; each castigates the lie and deception.

Is it any wonder, then, that the Brontë sisters are cult figures today? Their home, Haworth Parsonage, has been turned into a sacred precinct where countless visitors come to pay homage to the unique artists that were—Emily, Charlotte, and Anne.

The *mysteries* embedded in the use of symbols and images in their novels cast a spell. Esoteric (from the Greek *eisôtheô*, "I make enter"), their intention is to open the door, to make accessible what lies hidden and buried in darkness.

Notes

For publication information, see under Select Bibliography, pp. 191–93.

Introduction

1. *The Shakespeare Head Brontë: Life and Letters*, vol. 2, p. 363 (October 23, 1847, W. S. Williams).
2. Barbara and Gareth Lloyd Evans, *The Scribner Companion to the Brontës*, p. 372.
3. Ada Harrison and Derek Stanford, *Anne Brontë*, p. 227.
4. Ibid.
5. Herbert Reed, *The Meaning of Art*, p. 215.

Chapter 1: The Worlds of Branwell, Anne, Emily and Charlotte Brontë

1. Elizabeth Gaskell, *The Life of Charlotte Brontë*, pp. 3, 4, 28.
   Poetry extracts in this chapter drawn from Patrick Branwell Brontë, *The Poems of Patrick Branwell Brontë*, ed. Tom Winnifrith.

   The Poems of Anne Brontë: A New Text and Commentary, ed. Edward Chitham.

   Complete Poems of Emily Brontë, ed. C. W. Hatfield.

   The Poems of Charlotte Brontë, ed. Tom Winnifrith.
2. Rebecca Frazer, *The Brontës. Charlotte Brontë and Her Family*, p. 12.
3. *The Shakespeare Head Brontë: Life and Letters*, vol. 1, p. 18 (October 21, 1812, #8).
4. Ibid., p. 23 (December 5, 1812, #10).
5. Winifred Gérin, *Charlotte Brontë: The Evolution of Genius*, p. 15.
6. *The Shakespeare Head Brontë: The Miscellaneous and Unpublished Writing of Charlotte and Patrick Branwell Brontë*, vol. 1, p. 2.
7. Gaskell, p. 61.
8. Ibid., p. 68.
9. *Life and Letters*, vol. 1, p. 103 (July 21, 1832, #23, Ellen Nussey).

10. Gaskell, p. 81.
11. Ibid., p. 90.
12. Charlotte Brontë, quoted in preface to 1850 edition of *Wuthering Heights*. See Richard Benvenuto, *Emily Brontë*, p. 9.
13. *Life and Letters*, vol. 1, p. 140 (1836, #45, Ellen Nussey).
14. Gaskell, p. 110.
15. Ibid., p. 110.
16. Charlotte Brontë, *Five Novelettes*, p. 34.
17. Gaskell, p. 87.
18. Ibid., p. 88.
19. *Life and Letters*, vol. 1, p. 155 (March, 1837, #59, Robert Southey).
20. Gaskell, p. 97.
21. Ibid., p. 123.
22. *Life and Letters*, vol. 1, p. 239 (July 30, 1841); vol. 2, p. 52 (Anne's Diary).
23. *Life and Letters*, vol. 1, p. 250 (January 20, 1842).
24. Gaskell, p. 151.
25. Ibid.
26. Ibid., p. 147.
27. Gaskell, p. 159.
28. Gaskell, p. 160.
29. *Life and Letters*, vol. 1, p. 301 (August 6, 1843, #161, Ellen Nussey); vol. 1, p. 309 (December 19, 1843, #167, Emily).
30. *Life and Letters*, vol. 2, p. 13 (July 24, 1844, #179, Mr. Héger).
31. *Life and Letters*, vol. 1, p. 306 (October 13, 1843, #127, Ellen Nussey).
32. *Life and Letters*, vol. 2, p. 241 (July 31, 1848, #348, W. S. Williams).
33. Winifred Gérin, *Branwell Brontë*, p. 247 (Francis H. Grundy, October 1845).
34. Ibid., p. 254.
35. Ibid., p. 270.
36. Ibid., p. 297.
37. *Life and Letters*, vol. 2, p. 295 (December 25, 1848, #412, W. S. Williams).
38. *Life and Letters*, vol. 2, p. 317 (March 24, 1849, #431, Margaret Wooler).
39. *Life and Letters*, vol. 4, p. 4 (August 25, 1852).

Chapter 2: Patrick Branwell Brontë: Eternal Adolescent

1. Patrick Branwell Brontë, *The Poems of Patrick Branwell Brontë*, ed. Tom Winnifrith, p. 28. "Misery II." All poetry in this chapter is drawn from this edition.
2. Esther Harding, *Psychic Energy*, pp. 136–7.
3. Barbara Hannah, *Striving towards Wholeness*, p. 149.

4. Winifred Gérin, *Branwell Brontë*, p. 19.
5. *Legends of Angria*. Edited by Fannie E. Ratchford and William Clyde De Vane, p. 18.
6. Hannah, p. 151.
7. Barbara Evans and Lloyd Gareth, *The Scribner Companion to the Brontës*, p. 36.
8. Gérin, p. 40.
9. Ibid., p. 43.
10. Evans, p. 139, ("The Characters of Celebrated Men" 1829).
11. Ratchford, p. 23.
12. Evans, p. 140.
13. *Life and Letters*, vol. 1, p. 135 (April 8, 1836, #42).
14. Ibid., p. 151 (January 19, 1837, #57); 127 (May 8, 1835, #36, Ellen Nussey).
15. Gérin, p. 73.
16. Ibid., p. 83.
17. *Life and Letters*, vol. 2, p. 124 (January 24, 1847, #280, J. B. Leyland).
18. Francis H. Grundy was Branwell's friend after 1841.

Chapter 3: Anne Brontë: "Smouldering Fire"

1. *The Poems of Anne Brontë: A New Text and Commentary*, ed. Edward Chitham. "A dreadful darkness closes in," January 7, 1849. All poetry in this chapter is drawn from this edition.
2. *Life and Letters*, vol. 2, pp. 320–1 (April 5, 1849, #434, to Ellen Nussey). See P. J. M. Scott, *Anne Brontë: A New Critical Assessment*.
3. May Sinclair, *The Three Brontës*, p. 188.
4. Acton Bell, *The Tenant of Wildfell Hall*, vol. I, p. xi.
5. Ada Harrison and Derek Stanford, *Anne Brontë*, p. 227.
6. Anne Brontë, *Agnes Grey*. Edited with introduction and notes by Angeline Goreau, p. 61.
7. *Life and Letters*, vol. 1, p. 239, "Birthday Paper."
8. Winifred Gérin, *Anne Brontë*, p. 72.
9. Inga-Stina Ewbank, *Their Proper Sphere*, p. 64.
10. Barbara and Gareth Lloyd Evans, *The Scribner Companion to the Brontës*, p. 381. (January 1848; January 22, 1848).
11. Harrison and Stanford, p. 223.
12. Barbara Hannah, *Striving towards Wholeness*, p. 180.
13. Ibid., p. 183.
14. Evans and Evans, pp. 382, 384 (October 1848; August 1849).
15. Harrison and Stanford, p. 227.

Chapter 4: Emily Brontë: Locked in One's Own World

1. *Complete Poems of Emily Brontë*, ed. C. W. Hatfield, p. 55. All poetry in this chapter is from this edition.
2. Barbara Hannah, *Striving towards Wholeness*, p. 193.

3. Emily Dickinson, *Letters*, vol. 2, p. 844.
4. Mary Louise von Franz, *Timeless Documents of the Soul*, p. 79.
5. Mircea Eliade, *The Myth of the Eternal Return*, p. 29.
6. Hannah, pp. 193–200.
7. Ibid.
8. Ibid., p. 232.
9. Ibid., p. 246.
   See also Harold Bloom, Editor, *Emily Brontë's Wuthering Heights:* Dorothy Van Ghent, "On *Wuthering Heights*," pp. 9–26. Ann Smith, Ed. *The Art of Emily Brontë:* Robin Grove, " 'It Would Not Do': Emily Brontë as Poet." pp. 33–67; Rosalind Miles, "A Baby God: The Creative Dynamism of Emily Brontë's Poetry" pp. 68–93; Barbara Hardy, "The Lyricism of Emily Brontë" pp. 94–120; Keith Sagar, "The Originality of *Wuthering Heights*," pp. 121–159; J. F. Goodridge, "A New Heaven and a New Earth," pp. 160–181.

Chapter 5: Charlotte Brontë: "If You Knew My Thoughts. . . ."

1. *The Poems of Charlotte Brontë*, ed. Tom Winnifrith, p. 243. Poems quoted in this chapter from this edition.
2. *Life and Letters*, vol. 1, p. 139 (May 10, 1836).
3. C. G. Jung, *The Portable Jung*, p. 145.
4. Edward Edinger, "An Outline of Analytical Psychology," p. 10.
5. Earl A. Knies, *The Art of Charlotte Brontë*. From "Novels by the Authoress of 'John Halifax,' " *North British Review*, 29 (1858), pp. 474–475.
6. Erich Newmann, *The Place of Creation*, p. 136.
7. C. G. Jung, *Collected Works*, pp. 5, 281, 480, 436. Marie Louise von Franz, "Archetypes Surrounding Death, *Quadrant*, 5–23.
8. Ibid.
9. *Life and Letters*, vol. 2, p. 363 (October 23, 1847, W. S. Williams).
10. Barbara Hannah, *Striving towards Wholeness*, p. 141.
11. Miriam Allott, ed. *The Brontës: The Critical Heritage*, p. 165.
12. Laura L. Hinkley, *The Brontës: Charlotte and Emily*, p. 165.
13. L. Korg, "The Problem of Unity in *Shirley*," *Nineteenth-Century Fiction*, 12:2, 1957, p. 136.
14. Elizabeth Gaskell, *The Life of Charlotte Brontë*, pp. 387, 365.
15. Barbara and Gareth Lloyd Evans, *The Scribner Companion to the Brontës*, p. 372. (*Daily News*, February 3, 1853; *Letters to Mrs. Bray*, February 15, 1853; *Westminster Review*, April 1853; Letter to H. Clough, 1853).

Conclusion

1. *The Shakespeare Head Brontë: Life and Letters*, vol. 2, p. 184.
2. Herbert Reed, *The Meaning of Art*, p. 181.

Select Bibliography

Primary Sources:

The Shakespeare Head Brontë. Edited by T. J. Wise and J. A. Symington. 19 volumes. Oxford: The Shakespeare Head Press, 1931–38. (Novels, 11 volumes; Life and Letters, 4 volumes; Poems, 2 volumes; Miscellaneous and Unpublished Writings, 2 volumes.)

Legends of Angria. Edited by Fannie E. Ratchford and William Clyde De Vane. New Haven: Yale University Press, 1933.

The Twelve Adventurers and Other Stories. Edited by C. K. Shorter and C. W. Hatfield. London: Hodder and Stoughton, 1925.

Anne Brontë, *The Poems of Anne Brontë.* Edward Chitham, Editor. London: Macmillan, 1979.

——. *Agnes Grey.* Angeline Goreau, Editor. London: Penguin Books, 1988.

——. *The Tenant of Wildfell Hall.* 2 vols. Oxford: Shakespeare Head Press. Basil and Blackwell, 1931.

Charlotte Brontë, *The Poems of Charlotte Brontë.* Edited by Tom Winnifrith. London: Basil and Blackwell Pub., 1984.

——. *The Professor.* Edited by Margaret Smith and Herbert Rosengarten. Oxford: Clarendon Press, 1987.

——. *Shirley.* Introduction by Margaret Lane. New York: Dutton, Everyman's Library, 1975.

——. *Villette.* London: The Folio Society, 1967.

——. *Five Novelettes.* Edited by Winifred Gérin. London: The Folio Press, 1971.

Emily Brontë, *Complete Poems of Emily Brontë.* Edited by C. W. Hatfield. New York: Columbia University Press, 1941.

Emily Brontë, *Wuthering Heights.* Hilda Marsden and Ian Jack. Oxford: The Clarendon Press, 1978. New York: Pocket Books, Inc., 1939.

Patrick Branwell Brontë, *The Poems of Patrick Branwell Brontë.* Edited by Tom Winnifrith. New York: New York University Press, 1983.

Secondary Sources:

Allott, Miriam, ed. *The Brontës: The Critical Heritage*. London: Routledge and Kegan Paul, 1974.

Bentley, Phyllis, *The Brontës*. New York: The Viking Press, 1969.

Benvenuto, Richard, *Emily Brontë*. Boston: Twayne Publishers, 1982.

Bloom, Harold, Editor, *Modern Critical Views The Brontës*. New York: Chelsea House Publishers, 1987.

Bloom, Margaret, *Charlotte Brontë*. Boston: Twayne Publishers, 1977.

Chadwick, Mrs. Ellis H. *In the Footsteps of the Brontës*. London: Sir Isaac Pitman and Sons, 1914.

Chitham, Edward, *A Life of Emily Brontë*. London: Basil Blackwell, 1987.

Craik, W. A. *The Brontë Novels*. London: Methuen, 1971.

Dickinson, Emily, *The Letters of Emily Dickinson*. Edited by Thomas Johnson. 3 vols. Cambridge, MA: Harvard University Press, 1951, 1955.

Eliade, Mircea, *The Myth of the Eternal Return*. Princeton: Princeton University Press, 1974.

Ewbank, Inga-Stina, *Their Proper Sphere: A Study of the Brontë Sisters as Early Victorian Female Novelists*. London: Edward Arnold, 1966.

Evans, Barbara and Gareth Lloyd, *The Scribner Companion to the Brontës*. New York: Charles Scribner's Sons, 1982.

Franz, Marie Louise, von, "Archetypes Surrounding Death," *Quadrant*. Summer, 1979.

———. "The Dream of Descartes," *Timeless Documents of the Soul*. Evanston: Northwestern University Press, 1968.

Fraser, Rebecca, *The Brontës. Charlotte Brontë and Her Family*. New York: Crown Publishers, Inc., 1988.

Gaskell, E. [Elizabeth] C. *The Life of Charlotte Brontë*. London: Penguin, 1975.

Gérin, Winifred, *Anne Brontë*. London: Allen Lane, 1959.

———. *Branwell Brontë*. London: Radius Book/Hutchinson, 1972.

———. *The Life of Charlotte Brontë*. Oxford: Oxford University Press, 1967.

———. *Emily Brontë: A Biography*. Oxford: Clarendon Press, 1971.

Hannah, Barbara, *Striving towards Wholeness*. Boston: Sigo Press, 1988.

Hanson, Lawrence, and Hanson, E. M., *The Four Brontës: The Lives and Works of Charlotte, Branwell, Emily, and Anne Brontë*. London: Oxford University Press, 1949.

Harding, Esther, *The I and the Not I*. Princeton: Princeton University Press, 1973.

———. *Psychic Energy*. Princeton: Princeton University Press, 1973.

Harrison, Ada and Stanford, Derek, Anne Brontë. Archon Books, 1970.

Hewish, John. *Emily Brontë: A Critical and Biographical Study*. London: Macmillan and Co., 1969.

Hinkley, Laura L. *The Brontës: Charlotte and Emily.* London: Hammond and Co., 1947.

Jung, C. G., *Collected Works.* 1–20. Princeton: Princeton University Press, 1957–79.

Keefe, Robert, *Charlotte Brontë's World of Death.* Austin: University of Texas Press, 1979.

Knies, Earl A. *The Art of Charlotte Brontë.* Athens, Ohio: Ohio University Press, 1969.

Linder, Cynthia A., *Romantic Imagery in the Novels of Charlotte Brontë.* New York: Barnes and Noble, 1978.

Martin, Robert B., *Accents of Persuasion: Charlotte Brontë's Novels.* London: Faber and Faber, 1966.

Maurier, Daphne du, *The Infernal World of Branwell Brontë.* New York: Doubleday and Co., 1961.

Maynard, John, *Charlotte Brontë and Sexuality.* Cambridge: Cambridge University Press, 1984.

Miles, Rosalind, "A Baby God: The Creative Dynamism of Emily Brontë's Poetry." In *The Art of Emily Brontë.* Edited by Anne Smith. New York: Barnes and Noble, 1976.

Newman, Erich, *The Place of Creation.* Princeton: Princeton University Press, 1989.

Peters, Margot, *Charlotte Brontë: Style in the Novel.* Madison, Wisconsin: University of Wisconsin Press, 1973.

Pollard, Arthur, *Charlotte Brontë.* London: Routledge and Kegan Paul, 1968.

Ratchford, Fannie E., *The Brontës' Web of Childhood.* New York: Columbia University Press, 1941.

Scott, P. J. M., *Anne Brontë: A New Critical Assessment.* London: Vision and Barnes and Noble, 1983.

Showalter, Elaine, *A Literature of their Own: British Women Novelists from Brontë to Lessing.* London: Virago, 1982.

Sinclair, May, *The Three Brontës.* London: Hutchinson Co. Ltd., 1912.

Smith, Anne, ed., *The Art of Emily Brontë.* New York: Barnes and Noble, 1976.

Spark, Muriel, and Stanford, Derek, *Emily Brontë: Her Life and Work.* New York: Coward-McCann, 1966.

Winnifrith, T. J., *The Brontës and their Background: Romance and Reality.* London: Macmillan, 1973.

Index

This book may be kept

FOURTEEN DAYS

A fine will be charged for each day the book
is kept over time.